MENTAL ILLNESS

VOLUME 3 of 5

The Reality of the Physical Nature

by
Dr. Daniel R. Berger II

Mental Illness: The Reality of the Physical Nature, Volume 3

Library of Congress Control Number: 2016907654
Trade Paperback ISBN: 978-0-9864114-8-9
Cover Artwork by: Elieser Loewenthal
Edited by: Laurie Buck

Published by Alethia International Publications - Taylors, SC

www.drdanielberger.com

Printed in the United States of America.

To
Dr. Hugh Clarke
who spent a great portion
of his life operating on and helping
to heal the human brain, but who
will be most remembered for his
love for God and others.

TABLE OF CONTENTS

ACKNOWLEDGMENTS

This project was made possible by many friends, family, and professionals who sacrificed time and gave effort to read early drafts and offer me valuable feedback, conversations, and suggestions. Specifically, I would like to thank my wife, Oriana, and my parents, Dan and Gail Berger, who both patiently encouraged me through the several years of research and writing and engaged in useful discussions with me throughout the process. I wish to also thank a group of people that consists of several therapists, a neurosurgeon, a functional neurologist, pastors, a former psychiatrist, and others with medical backgrounds: Laura Beauvais, Ethan Stanley, Dr. Christina Biester, Trudy Fremont, Dr. Hugh Clarke, Tim Lovegrove, Dr. Kevin Hurt, Dr. Joe Henson, Dr. Elliot Hirshorn, Dr. Gregg Mazak, Douglas Phillips, and John Hutchison, Jr. Additionally, Gayle and Marcy Broughton, James Moran, and Jeff Clemens contributed valuable insight and discussion along the way. Likewise, the hard work of my editor, Laurie Buck, has been essential to the final product. Finally, I want to thank all the individuals and families who over the past many years have allowed me to be a small part of their lives in offering them Scriptural answers that enable them to have life more abundantly and to progress in allowing God to renew their mind.

DISCLAIMER

The material contained in this book is the result of years of experience, research, and professional interviews, but it is not intended in any way to be taken as medical advice. Rather, the views and material expressed in this book are philosophical and historical in nature and written in order to provide truth and hope that will enable pastors, clinicians, therapists, counselors, university professors, and other professionals to be better equipped to offer genuine truth, love, and hope to those in their care.

ABBREVIATIONS

ANS	Autonomic Nervous System
APA	American Psychiatric Association
ADHD	Attention Deficit-Hyperactivity Disorder
CBS	Charles Bonnet Syndrome
DSM-5	*Diagnostic & Statistical Manual of Mental Disorders – 5*
ECT	Electroconvulsive Therapy
EEG	Electroencephalogram
EMDR	Eye Movement Desensitization & Reprocessing Therapy
EF	Executive Function
ES	Executive System
ESV	*English Standard Version*
FMRI	Functional Magnetic Resonance Imaging
JAMA	*Journal of the American Medical Association*
NAMI	National Alliance for the Mentally Ill
NEJM	*New England Journal of Medicine*
NIH	National Institutes of Health
NIMH	National Institute of Mental Health
PNI	Psychonueroimmunology
TMS	Transcranial Magnetic Stimulation
CNS	Central Nervous System

BOOK SERIES

This book is one volume of five in a series on the current construct of mental illness. Each volume builds upon the other in a logical and progressive explanation. Although each volume can be read separately and out of order, following the designed order will provide the most benefit to the reader.

INTRODUCTION

"The illuminated brain cannot be trusted to offer an unfiltered view of the mind. Nor is it logical to regard behavior as beyond an individual's control simply because the associated neural mechanisms can be shown to be 'in the brain.'"[1] –Sally Satel, psychiatrist, and Scott Lilienfeld, psychologist

"We have hunted for big simple neurochemical explanations for psychiatric disorders and have not found them."[2] – Dr. Kenneth S. Kendler, chief editor of *Psychological Medicine*

The dualism of human nature demands that we exclude neither the spiritual nor the physical in our efforts to understand and heal the mind. The shift in this discussion from the spiritual (volume 2)[3] to the physical may be considered by some to be a step from conjecture to hard observable science, but the reality is that the complexities of the body and its relationship to the immaterial mind will also demand faith.

In fact, to believe that alleged mental illnesses are caused by the physical nature requires faith. Drs. Stuart Kirk, Tomi Gomory, and David Cohen explain,

---

[1] Sally Satel and Scott Lilienfeld, *Brainwashed: The Seductive Appeal of Mindless Neuroscience* (New York: Basic Books, 2013), 150.

[2] Kenneth S. Kendler quoted by Jeffery Lacasse and Jonathan Leo, "Serotonin and Depression: A Disconnect between the Advertisements and the Scientific Literature," *PloS Medicine Journal* 2 (2005): 1211-16.

[3] Daniel R. Berger II, *Mental Illness: The Reality of the Spiritual Nature* (Taylors, SC: Alethia International Publications, 2016).

Many, perhaps a majority of adults today, believe that the problem of mental illness is fundamentally a medical problem whose solution lies, through conventional medical research, in identifying its causes and devising effective treatments (e.g., targeting brains and genes). Most people view modern drug treatments as an undisputed improvement (more effective and safer) over any previous interventions designed for those considered mentally ill. Moreover, many people believe (or perhaps merely hope) that those labeled severely mentally ill—and those who treat them—now operate in an atmosphere of cooperation without the use [of] coercion.[4]

Faith is necessary because every approach to the mind, its genuine struggles, and how it relates to the brain all require a guiding presuppositional worldview. For example, Dr. Panksepp reveals that his own approach to mental illness is based upon the theory of evolution: "The logo of [his] book reflects this philosophy of recognizing that the multiple layers of brain/mind evolution are reflected in the *evolutionary* passages which serve as a foundation for the human mind."[5] Panksepp's view—and that of most of his secular colleagues—holds that the mind is evolved material or merely a byproduct of the physical brain. Thus the current secular ideology marginalizes the spiritual mind as secondary to the brain or as an extension of the brain and chooses instead to focus its attention on the body—specifically genes, chemicals of the brain, and the nervous system. The claim is simple: the physical nature controls mindsets, emotions, and behavior, even those that are moral in nature. This tenet of materialism seemingly enables evolutionists to explain away the spiritual nature, to attribute the mind's control over the body to the brain, to suggest that science and medicine possess the answers to people's genuine mental

---

[4] Stuart Kirk, Tomi Gomory, and David Cohen, *Mad Science: Psychiatric Coercion, Diagnosis, and Drugs* (New Brunswick, NJ: Transaction Publishers, 2013), preface viii.

[5] Jaak Panksepp, ed. *Textbook of Biological Psychiatry*, (Hoboken, NJ: John Wiley and Sons, 2004), 2.

struggles, and to dismiss morality and responsibility as archaic and unscientific thinking.

But is the issue of mental illness a scientific study at all? It is important to reiterate from volumes 1 and 2 that the mind is neither matter nor the byproduct of matter that can be approached using the scientific method. Philosophy, theology, sociology, and religion are the true vehicles of discussion whenever the mind is studied and described. In contrast, neurons, neural connections, genetics, and natural bodily chemicals (e.g. serotonin) can somewhat be observed, studied, and claimed to be the source of behavior when changes occur. But these repeatable and observable biological phenomena can just as easily be explained as physiological effects of the brain produced by the mind if a different faith is held. Psychiatrist Peter Breggin explains,

> Common sense and experimental evidence indicate that certain passionate states are associated with corresponding changes in brain function. Prolonged mental stresses of almost any kind, as well as psychical trauma or stress, cause the brain to stimulate increased production of certain hormones, such as steroids. Conversely, if you are relaxing right now, your steroid output may decline. *In each of these instances the mental state influenced the brain, rather than vice versa.* We find the same results examining brain waves. If you are excited with intense focus of your attention, your brain is likely to generate fast low-amplitude electrical waves on the electroencephalogram (EEG). If you then relax, the EEG will show alpha waves — slower, with a higher amplitude in each case, *the mental state influenced how the brain reacted, not vice versa* [emphasis added].[6]

Likewise, cognitive neuroscientist Caroline Leaf remarks,

> The brain responds to your mind by sending these neurological signals throughout the body, which means that your thoughts and emotions are transformed into physiological and spiritual effects, and then physiological experiences transform into mental and emotional states. It's a profound and eye-opening thought to realize

---

[6] Peter R. Breggin, *Toxic Psychiatry* (New York: St. Martin's Press, 1991), 112.

something seemingly immaterial like a belief can take on a physical existence as a positive or negative change in our cells.[7]

Scientists are unable to observe or measure the non-physical mind, but they can observe the mind's effects on the body and form corresponding theories according to their beliefs. Brain-dysfunction advocates, though, insist that these physical changes equal mental illness rather than recognizing that these biological changes could just as easily be explained as the spiritual mind's effects on the physical body.

We must also make it clear at the outset of this volume that effects do not equal causes, and causes and effects are regularly confused and not easily determined when discerning correlations between the mind and the brain. If science is the primary or only tool used to study physical phenomenon such as behavior, then rightly determining causes and effects will also be limited to only that which is discovered through physical observation. Researcher and professor of medicine Dr. Bruce Lipton remarks of this common occurrence within the media: "Confusion occurs when the media repeatedly distort the meaning of two words: correlation and causation. It's one thing to be linked to a disease; it's quite another to cause a disease, which implies a directing, controlling action."[8] The brain's correlation to the mind is undeniable, but whether or not the brain is the chief executive of all behavior is in question. Does the brain influence the mind, does it control the mind, or is it rather controlled and altered by the mind? Answers to these questions are matters of faith; that is, they spring from an

---

[7] Caroline Leaf, *Switch on Your Brain: The Key to Peak Happiness, Thinking, and Health* (Grand Rapids: Baker, 2013), 14.

[8] Bruce H. Lipton, *The Biology of Belief: Unleashing the Power of Consciousness, Matter and Miracles* (New York: Hay House, 2005), 21.

interpretation of empirical evidence according to an established worldview.

Volume 2 of this series established that the mind cannot be observed or tested through scientific experiments;[9] thus, psychology — the study of the mind — is not a true science of the mind. It makes sense, then, why brain-dysfunction theorists and neuroscientists prefer to focus their attention on the physical brain and observable behavior rather than attempt to apply the scientific process to research the immaterial mind.

Furthermore, we discussed that the foundational requirement of faith to approach and define the reality of the mind makes its study and understanding impossible solely through the lens of science or by researching the brain. Drs. Sally Satel and Scott Lilienfeld (who are both determinists) comment that "one cannot use the physical rules from the cellular level to completely predict activity at the psychological level."[10] In other words, understanding the brain is not equal to understanding the immaterial mind, and understanding the brain's involvement in human activity and even our ability to view neuroimages is not the same as observing the spiritual mind and its thoughts or even discovering causes of neural activity. FMRIs and EEGs, which produce images of the physical brain, do not produce images of the spiritual mind — a point we will examine further in the chapters to come.

No human tool including the scientific process can observe the immaterial nature of mankind. Instead, we must discern things about our spiritual nature and the spiritual world from that which is spiritual — namely God's Holy Word — and (from a

---

[9] Berger, *Mental Illness: Spiritual Nature.*

[10] Satel and Lilienfeld, *Brainwashed,* introduction xvi.

limited perspective) that which is observable in the natural world. In truth, scientific research cannot evaluate, deny, test, or explain the reality of the human spiritual nature or even God Himself:

> Such a dualist arrangement must be taken on faith and, like the existence of a godlike entity, cannot be disproved by science. This is because scientific inquiry depends on observation of measurable events that take place in the natural world; its purpose is to illuminate cause-and-effect relationships and test predictions based on them. As part of the supernatural realm, immaterial souls and a transcendent God are not amenable to the tools of science. So this strategy is a scientific dead end.[11]

Dr. Bruce Lipton also asserts,

> Spirit and other metaphysical concepts were devalued as "unscientific" because their truths could not be assessed by the analytic methods of science. The important "stuff" about life and the Universe became the domain of rational scientists.[12]

The only way materialists can discuss the mind/soul in scientific terms and contexts is by reducing it to somehow be physical in nature—a part or byproduct of the brain—or by outright denying its relevance over executive moral controls. So when psychiatrists and other secularists speak of the physical nature in regards to mental health, terms and concepts are often blurred between what is truly science, such as the study of the nervous system, and what is merely scientism, which is faith in science alone to explain even the unobservable.

Logically, then, when a person—no matter what his degrees or clinical experience—claims to possess a scientific explanation or theory of the mind and proceeds to explain the mind using biological terms and concepts, one should discern immediately that such a proposed theory is actually scientism (faith in the

---

[11] Ibid., 130.

[12] Lipton, *Biology of Belief,* 158.

scientific process) and not validated or measureable science. Additionally, such a suggestion indicates that materialism and reductionism are the root philosophical beliefs and not the scientific process.

Attempting to understand the brain-mind connection through science alone is a dead end. Discerning our true nature cannot be done apart from special revelation (the Bible) and natural revelation (the material world — usually approached by the scientific process). Both of these important realities help people to understand true anthropology and theology and are never contradictory.

But even the scientific method is limited in observing and understanding the brain, and neuroscientists must still rely on foundational faith to form theories and to fill in the many unknowns. Dr. Peter Gray explains,

> Neuroscientists have made much-touted progress in understanding the brain, but still that understanding is extremely superficial. We have no idea, really, how the brain does any of the amazing things it does (beyond the simplest reflexes), but we do have some ideas about which parts of the brain are most involved in which functions.[13]

Dr. Frances also remarks,

> No doubt there is an enormous gap between things as they really are and things as we perceive them — and not just in psychiatry. Only 4 percent of our known universe can be directly detected by our senses — the rest of this energy and matter remaining "dark" to us.[14]

---

[13] Peter Gray, "The 'ADHD Personality': Its Cognitive, Biological, and Evolutionary Foundations," http://www.psychologytoday.com/blog/freedom-learn/201008/the-adhd-personality-its-cognitive-biological-and-evolutionary-foundations.

[14] Allen Frances, *Saving Normal: An Insider's Revolt against Out-of-Control Psychiatric Diagnosis, DSM-5, Big Pharma, and the Medicalization of Ordinary Life* (New York: HarperCollins, 2013), 20.

So while biological psychiatrists and many other medical professionals are confident that mental illness is a matter of biology and that anthropology can be rightly and fully explained through social sciences and medicine, the discerning believer will know that these claims are simply unverified speculations born out of a worldview based on faith.[15] In fact, as we will observe in this volume and those to come, much of what is claimed to be science in the secular construct of mental illness often amounts to unproven — though thoroughly researched and published — speculation.[16]

The mind is not physical and cannot be subjected to the scientific process, but much of the physical body can be approached through the scientific method. Since the brain, its chemicals, and neural connections along with the study of genes are the central objects in the secular construct, most of our discussion will be centered on these aspects of human physicality, the many theories that surround them, and the tools available to study them. While there is much unknown about the human psychosomatic nature, we can conclude from the evidence that we do possess what is true and false about people. Theories which are found to be false by empirical evidence or for which exceptions exist, however, must be denounced, distrusted, and recognized as invalid. What will emerge from this study on the physical nature is that the brain-dysfunction theory — the core of Emil Kraepelin's theory and the foundation of the current construct of mental illness — is not only speculative, but it is also a false faith that conflicts with empirical evidence.

---

[15] Charles L. Whitfield, *The Truth about Mental Illness: Choices for Healing* (Deerfield Beach, FL: Health Communications, 2004), preface xvi.

[16] Lipton, *Biology of Belief*, 21-22.

After establishing a definition of normalcy, deciding corresponding authority, determining whether mankind has a dual nature or a mono nature, and defining the human mind, we must then answer several pressing questions in this volume. The answers to these questions will reflect the position of an established authority, a presuppositional worldview, and be able to provide reliable conclusions across social sciences and cultures. The questions that we will explore in this volume are: (1) Are people moral? (2) If so, what are behaviors that are moral and amoral? (3) Who is privileged to decide these distinctions? (4) Is the mind or is the brain the chief executive over these moral actions? (5) Can brain damage, impairment, or deterioration ever cause someone to behave immorally? (6) Is science (the study of matter or things which are physical, repeatable, and observable) a moral or amoral endeavor? (7) Is science the best tool to provide answers to mental struggles? (8) Is there any empirical evidence that invalidates the brain-dysfunction and genetic theories? Answers to these questions will provide a better understanding of our true psychosomatic nature.

CHAPTER 1 – THE MORAL NATURE OF SCIENCE

Since most psychiatrists, psychologists, and other medical professionals claim that science provides the greatest tool to yield insight and understanding of both the mind and the physical nature, understanding the moral nature of science becomes a logical starting point for our discussion. The false presuppositions that mental struggles are best understood through the scientific process and the incorrect conclusion that secular theories of the mind are scientifically valid and reliable represent major tenets of faith in the brain-dysfunction theory (the medical model) that must be examined. In fact, the belief in scientism to approach the mind is a direct result of Kraepelinian theory/biological psychiatry, and it has convinced many Christians either that Scripture does not speak to humanity's physical nature or that the Bible is subservient to secular scientific theory regarding the mind-brain connection.

In many ways, society in general and most secular professionals in particular have established science as the highest value and the most efficient tool in understanding human mental struggles and impairments. This belief in science may be due to the fact that many consider science to be truth or at least be the search for truth. But science does not equal truth nor does science possess truth; rather science is merely one's philosophy, approach, and interpretation of existing physical realities.

In fact, sciences — especially fields that claim to study the mind and human behavior — are moral endeavors. Renowned psychiatrist and historian Robert Lifton explains,

> Psychological research is always a moral enterprise, just as moral judgments inevitably include psychological assumptions. . . . Otto Rank had long been preoccupied with ethical principles he believed Freud and others had excluded from psychological work, largely because psychology itself was entrapped in its own scientific ideology"[17]

Science seems to be objective, but science is always dependent upon the morality of the individual(s) conducting the research and the worldview and integrity of the person interpreting the objective data. In other words, science is only as morally sound as the person practicing it and forming the conclusions.

Understanding the Secular Paradigm of Science

To better understand why science is given such preeminence we must realize the moral nature of science, and discovering the purpose behind secular research helps this understanding. When most secular professionals speak of making their theories more scientific, they are not advocating that the construct of mental illness be more in line with truth nor do they purpose to discover truth,[18] but rather they most often seek to conform their research, observations, and conclusions to their materialistic/evolutionary ideology. Evolutionary biologist and geneticist at Harvard University, Richard Lewontin, explains,

> Our willingness to accept scientific claims that are against common sense is the key to an understanding of the real struggle between science and the supernatural. We take the side of science is spite of the patent absurdity of some of its constructs, in spite of its failure to fulfill many of its extravagant promises of health and life, in spite of the tolerance of the scientific community of unsubstantiated just so stories, because we have a prior commitment, a commitment to materialism. It is not that the methods of and institutions of science somehow compel us to accept a material explanation of the phenomenal world, but on the contrary, that we are forced by our a priori adherence to material causes to create an apparatus of

---

[17] Robert Jay Lifton, *The Nazi Doctors: Medical Killing and the Psychology of Genocide* (New York: Basic Books, 1986), 12-13.

[18] Frances, *Saving Normal*, 21.

investigation and a set of concepts that produce material explanations, no matter how counterintuitive, no matter how mystifying to the uninitiated. *Moreover, that materialism is absolute, for we cannot allow a Divine Foot in the door* [emphasis added]."[19]

Secular science is most often not a pursuit of truth, and some prominent scientists even admit that their scientific endeavors — in accordance with their "priori adherence" or worldview — are merely attempts to keep God out of any explanation of the natural world. In short, the secular concept of science is an "apparatus" designed to suppress the truth of God revealed in His creation of the natural world. Science is not a search or discovery for truth, but a new explanation of truth in order to deny the one who is true. In the same way that Dr. Lewontin describes science, Romans 1:18-20 explains the same human tendency:

> For the wrath of God is revealed from heaven against all ungodliness and unrighteousness of men, who by their unrighteousness suppress the truth. For what can be known about God is plain to them, because God has shown it to them. For his invisible attributes, namely, his eternal power and divine nature, have been clearly perceived, ever since the creation of the world, in the things that have been made. So they are without excuse.

The proposed science underlying and surrounding the construct of mental illness is an attempt to explain away God and establish an elaborate excuse. This is not merely a Scriptural perspective, but a prominent secular one as well. Furthermore, both perspectives reveal that the science of mental illness is dependent entirely upon one's faith and worldview.

The necessity of faith to approach science was expressed by the science historian Thomas Kuhn in 1962 when he coined the

---

[19] Richard C. Lewontin, "Billions and Billions of Demons," *New York Review of Books* (January 7, 1997): 31.

term *paradigm* in his book *The Structure of Scientific Revolutions.*[20] Kuhn asserted that the word *paradigm* best describes this closed-minded approach or belief system that people erect in order to define and interpret the natural world. "Science" then, represents an individually or socially constructed moral religious system and not objective fact or truth. Dr. Abramson explains,

> Kuhn coined the term "paradigm" to describe the unspoken professional values, beliefs, and techniques shared by a community of scientists or professionals. The shared paradigm then defines the range of problems that are legitimate to investigate, the range of legitimate solutions, and the criteria that justify belief that the findings are true. Particularly during all the years of intense medical training, the *unspoken principles of biomedicine are communicated and enforced by the well-defined and ever-present structure of authority* [emphasis added].[21]

Likewise, Dr. Whitfield remarks,

> In his classic book on the dynamics of scientific revolutions, science historian Thomas Kuhn (1960) described a key characteristic of believers in a dominant scientific paradigm (i.e., belief system): they ask only those questions which confirm the dominant paradigm's central assumptions.[22]

Many secularists assert that science is "the search for truth,"[23] but evolutionary psychology blurs the lines between what is true and what is hoped or believed to be true. In actuality, their brand of science — which they cling to so tenaciously — is a social

---

[20] Thomas Kuhn, *The Structure of Scientific Revolutions*, 3rd ed. (Chicago: University of Chicago Press, 1996 first published in 1962).

[21] John Abramson, *Overdosed America: The Broken Promise of American Medicine* (New York: Harper Perennial, 2005), 202.

[22] Whitfield, *Truth about Mental Illness*, 174.

[23] Candace B. Pert, *Molecules of Emotion: The Science Behind Mind-Body Medicine* (New York: Scribner, 1997), 314.

and moral construct that attempts to describe God's natural and supernatural truths through the lens of evolutionary ideology. Science, therefore, does not equal objective truth, and many times does not even represent a search for truth. Within mental health, this means that at all costs, materialism/the brain-dysfunction theory must be upheld.

In regards to the science of mental health, most researchers and secular scientists do not desire to discover truth about the nature of the mind, but rather their efforts are an attempt to justify and defend their theories of materialism and evolution. Neuroscientist Jay Joseph quotes George Albee:

> "It is more accurate to say that they select theories that are consistent with their personal values, attitudes, and prejudices, and then go out into the world, or into the laboratory, to seek facts that validate their beliefs about the world and human nature, neglecting or denying observations that contradict their personal prejudices."[24]

Dr. Ramachandran also realizes that many secularists are not really after scientific discovery but are instead after abstracting information from research that they can fit into their worldview.[25] Dr. Abramson comments on how Thomas Kuhn recognized the same problem:

> Kuhn's most important contribution was to show that what appears from the outside to be the unrestricted pursuit of scientific discovery is really the result of scientific inquiry within a tightly restricted field. Facts that don't fit the current paradigm, like the greater reduction of the risk of heart disease by lifestyle changes than by Statin therapy, are discounted and ignored: "not real medicine," and "not what real doctors do."[26]

---

[24] Jay Joseph, *The Gene Illusion* (London: PCCS Books, 2003).

[25] V.S. Ramachandran and Sandra Blakeslee, *Phantoms in the Brain: Probing the Mysteries of the Human Mind* (New York: William Morrow and Company, 1998), 222.

[26] Abramson, *Overdosed America*, 202.

Science — especially the science of mental illness — is a moral endeavor sourced in one's faith. When people begin to approach the natural world, their faith concerning our origin ultimately determines their explanations and approaches to the entire natural world.[27] This truth is revealed in Hebrews 11:1-5:

> Now faith is the assurance of things hoped for, the conviction of things not seen. For by it the people of old received their commendation. *By faith we understand that the universe was created by the word of God, so that what is seen was not made out of things that are visible* [emphasis added].

How secular scientists respond when the scientific process yields discovered truths which disprove their false theories or rest outside of their constructs further reveals the moral nature of science. Dr. Ramachandran remarks on the possible reactions that scientists have to such a discovery and the commonality of their immoral responses:

> Sometimes the new observation simply doesn't fit. It is an "anomaly," inconsistent with the existing structure. The scientist can then do one of three things. First, he can ignore the anomaly, sweeping it under the carpet — a *form of psychological "denial" that is surprisingly common even among eminent researchers.* Second, scientists can make minor adjustments to the paradigm, trying to fit the anomaly into their worldview, and this would still be a form of normal science. Or they can generate ad hoc auxiliary hypotheses that sprout like so many branches from a single tree. But soon these branches become so thick and numerous that they threaten to topple the tree itself. Finally, they can tear down the edifice and create a completely new one that bears very little resemblance to the original.

---

[27] "For the critical attitude is not so much opposed to the dogmatic attitude as super-imposed upon it: criticism must be directed against existing and influential beliefs in need of critical revision — in other words, dogmatic beliefs. A critical attitude needs for its raw material, as it were, theories or beliefs which are held more or less dogmatically. Thus science must begin with myths, and with the criticism of myths" (Karl Popper, *Philosophy of Science: An Historical Anthology*, ed. by Timothy McGrew, Marc Alsperctor-Kelly, and Fritz Allhoff [New York: Wiley and Sons, 2009], 480).

This is what Kuhn called a "paradigm shift" or scientific revolution [emphasis added].[28]

Too often, as Ramachandran notes, many secular researchers choose to sweep truth under the rug and deny reality in order to save their theory and hold to their worldview. This practice is normative in the "science" which maintains the construct of mental illness. Professors of Sociology, Dr. Stuart Kirk, Tomi Gomory, and David Cohen, remark,

> Much of the psychiatric research that has fueled the expansion of the mental health enterprise has not contributed to a science of madness. Instead, it has fueled mad science, which rests on unverified concepts, the invention of new forms of coercion, unremitting disease mongering, the widespread use of treatments with poorly tested and misleading claims of effectiveness, and rampant conflicts of interest that have completely blurred science and marketing. This is the "madness" of American psychiatry, and of psychiatry in much of the world.[29]

Likewise, clinical instructor at Harvard Medical School, Dr. John Abramson comments,

> Within the FDA, the doctors, scientists, and statisticians are dedicated to making sure the data about drugs and medical devices presented by manufacturers justify their claims of safety and efficacy.[30]

Applying the scientific process, believing in scientism, and forming conclusions about empirical findings all require a guiding moral system and agenda. For much of the research in the construct of mental illness, the goal is not to arrive at truth, but to support materialism, the brain-dysfunction and genetic theories, and ultimately the evolutionary worldview.

---

[28] Ramachandran and Blakeslee, *Phantoms in the Brain,* 222.

[29] Kirk, Gomory, and Cohen, *Mad Science,* preface ix.

[30] Abramson, *Overdosed America,* 85.

For a clinician or researcher who realizes the lack of empirical evidence to support his or her worldview, to reject the brain-dysfunction theory and make an about-face would be difficult; it is far easier to maintain the status quo and ignore discovered truths than to admit that you are wrong and have to change your entire paradigm. Dr. Ramachandran explains,

> With all this evidence staring them in the face, why do practitioners of Western medicine continue to ignore the many striking examples of direct links between mind and body? To understand why, it helps to have a feel for how scientific knowledge progresses. Most of the day-to-day progress of science depends on simply adding another brick to the great edifice—a rather humdrum activity that the late historian Thomas Kuhn called "normal science." *This corpus of knowledge, incorporating a number of widely accepted beliefs, is, in each instance, called a "paradigm."* Year after year new observations come along and are assimilated into an existing standard model. Most scientists are bricklayers, not architects; they are happy simply adding another stone to the cathedral. But sometimes the new observation simply doesn't fit [emphasis added].[31]

Secularists' wide-acceptance of the current construct of mental illness merely reflects their faith but does not validate their reductionistic beliefs.

It is important to reiterate that scientific conclusions are always a reflection of a person's worldview. Dr. Russell Barkley explains his own evolutionary ideology in regards to the psychiatric label of ADHD:

> Since we ask not for perfection [truth], but utility, we seek to build a ship that can be floated to be tested and revised, enabling us to build an even better ship that can be floated, tested, revised, and so on. Theories, like all accumulated information, are Darwinian in nature, evolving as their conceptual feet are held to empirical fires of experimentation, falsifiability, and revision.[32]

---

[31] V.S. Ramachandran and Sandra Blakeslee, *Phantoms in the Brain: Probing the Mysteries of the Human Mind* (New York: William Morrow and Company, 1998), 221-22.

[32] *NoSC*, 361.

Barkley confesses that his definition of science — which shapes his definition of mental illness — is not about discovering facts but rather pursuing justification for his beliefs, hopes, and opinions. Once again we see utilitarianism as the most important guide to anthropology in secular ideology. The moral nature of utilitarianism and its rejection of immutable truth is claimed to be science, but as the professor of psychiatry Thomas Szasz explains, it is, in truth, scientism:

> For the past century or so, psychologists have considered themselves, and have been accepted by others, as empirical scientists whose methods and theories are ostensibly the same as those of the biologists or physicist. Yet the fact remains that insofar as psychologists address themselves to the questions posed above, their work differs significantly from that of the natural scientist. *Psychologists and psychiatrists deal with moral problems* which, I believe, they cannot solve by medical methods [emphasis added].[33]

Evolutionary science is a moral paradigm, and as Szasz rightly notes, the secular brand of mental health science and its corresponding biological approaches to the human mind are attempts to heal the moral human nature through biomedicine.

The psychiatric practice of hiding their true faith beyond the façade of science has led to much confusion and deception and is anything but valid or reliable. Well-regarded neurologist V.S. Ramachandran explains,

> The distinction between fact and fiction gets more easily blurred in evolutionary psychology than in any other discipline, a problem that is exacerbated by the fact that most "ev-psych" [evolutionary psychology] explanations are completely untestable: You can't run experiments to prove or disprove them.[34]

While science and medicine are claimed to have the answers to the human soul, no one apart from God can observe the spiritual

---

[33] Thomas Szasz, *The Myth of Psychotherapy: Mental Healing as a Religion, Rhetoric, and Repression* (New York: Anchor Press, 1978), 9.

[34] Ramachandran and Blakeslee, *Phantoms in the Brain*, 202.

soul or mind. Many secular professionals in the mental health field recognize humanity's limitations and misguided attempts to approach the mind through scientific means:

> I will argue that the main problem faced by modern psychiatric services is not one of personnel or resources (although these may be important) but one of ideas. I will suggest that we have been laboring under serious misunderstandings about the nature of madness for more than a century, and that many contemporary approaches to the problem, although cloaked with the appearance of scientific rigor, have more in common with astrology than rational science. Only by abolishing these misunderstandings can we hope to improve the lot of the most impoverished, neglected and vulnerable of our citizens.[35]

The brand of science that allegedly approaches mental illness is really scientism that believes in the moral teachings of men like Darwin and Kraepelin. Historian Edward Shorter explains,

> Biological thinking gave psychiatry at the end of the twentieth century the capacity to be as science-driven as the rest of medicine. But this promise has remained unfulfilled, a result to psychiatry's enmeshment in popular values, in corporate culture, and in a boggy swamp of diagnostic scientism. . . . The psychiatry of everyday affliction has tended to lose its way.[36]

It is not merely believing in theories — though that somewhat summarizes scientism — but believing in the scientific process and human wisdom to interpret data. In many people's minds science is the highest form of truth and able to deliver humanity from its greatest problems. Former president of the American Medical Association, Dr. Louis Orr indentified this belief in 1958 when he stated that "Americans have come to believe that

---

[35] Richard Bentall, *Madness Explained: Psychosis and Human Nature* (New York: Penguin, 2003), 8.

[36] Edward Shorter, *A History of Psychiatry: From the Era of the Asylum to the Age of the Prozac* (New York: John Wiley & Sons, 1997), 288.

science is capable of almost everything."[37] Likewise, Dr. Abramson asserts,

> Could it be that, although we define our era by the tremendous scientific and technological progress that is being made (particularly in medicine), our desire to believe in this narrative of biomedical progress predisposes us to uncritical belief in its real merits? *In other words, might the shared belief in the potential of medical science be, in large part, our cultural mythology?* We tend to look upon myths with romantic condescension as the stories of primitive societies that provide shared meaning and hope and ease the prospect of suffering and death — stories that are made of "facts" that we (scientifically sophisticated as we are) know are not really true. Our belief that we are too scientifically grounded to succumb to such non-rational beliefs may, in fact, be our myth. . . . *These are our myths, merging science and hope into our shared belief* [emphasis added].[38]

Those who choose to rely on science for the care of the soul are placing their faith in the religion of scienticism. In fact, this is the religion necessary to believe that the brain is responsible for the mind's impairment and failures; one cannot have faith in the construct of mental illness without having faith in its proposed science. Secular researcher in physiology, biophysics, and former chief of brain biochemistry at the National Institutes of Health,[39] Dr. Candace Pert, exemplifies this common scientism:

> I have come to believe that science, at its very core, is a spiritual endeavor. Some of my best insights have come to me through what I can only call a mystical process. It's like having God whisper in your ear.[40]

Science is a construct that can only be approached by faith. If belief or faith is important to the scientific process, then not all

---

[37] Louis Orr quoted by James Harvey Young, *The Medical Messiahs* (Princeton, NJ: Princeton University Press, 1967), 281.

[38] Abramson, *Overdosed America*, 202.

[39] Pert, *Molecules of Emotion*, 14.

[40] Ibid., 315.

scientific theory, research, or conclusions in the mental health field are justifiable as dogma or reliable. In fact, Drs. Kutchins and Kirk note,

> In each new revision the claim is made that the [*DSM*] has achieved greater validity and more precision. Every change, even ones that are abandoned within a few months, is presented as a science-guided decision in which mistakes have been corrected, ambiguities have been clarified, and new knowledge has been incorporated. And since the final product, incorporating hundreds of minor and major changes, is never directly tied through citations to research articles, the claims of science-at-work are difficult to verify or dispute.[41]

Similarly, Edward Shorter comments,

> Science wanders astray easily in the world of quotidian anxiety and sadness, in the obsessive trails of behavior and the misfiring personality types that are the lot of humankind. Here the genetic trail grows dim and the neurotransmitters evaporate. Biology counts for little, culture and socialization for lots. Perhaps there are many separate disorders in this domain of neurotic illness, perhaps only a few, or none. The edges of this kind of psychiatry are poorly delineated, the boundaries between pathology and eccentricity vague. Despite its anchoring in the rest of medicine, psychiatry could easily drift aimlessly here.[42]

Many researchers are not after proving their theory which they dogmatically hold; instead, they desire to denounce any moral system that opposes their own. Dr. Thomas Szasz explains,

> The integrity of the natural scientific enterprise depends on truth-seeking and truth-speaking by individuals engaged in activities we call "scientific," and on the scientific commitment to expose and reject erroneous explanations and false "facts." In contrast, the stability of religions and the ersatz faiths of psychiatry and the so-called behavioral sciences depends on the loyalty of its practitioners

---

[41] Herb Kutchins and Stuart A. Kirk, *Making us Crazy* (New York: Free Press, 1997), 37-38.

[42] Edward Shorter, *A History of Psychiatry: From the Era of the Asylum to the Age of the Prozac* (New York: John Wiley & Sons, 1997), 288.

to established doctrines and institutions and the rejection of truth-telling as injurious to the welfare of the group that rest on it.[43]

If they cannot prove their theory to be true, they will do all they can to attack or dismiss any other possibility of describing the natural world. Dr. Whitfield remarks,

> Key in this erroneous thinking lies people's tendency to remain locked in a closed-circuit cycle that perpetuate their not considering all possible causes, which is the opposite of real science. In a strange kind of collective "thought disorder" themselves, they appear to be unable to think "outside of the box."[44]

Dr. Whitfield notes correctly that this delusional thinking that excludes truth in favor for belief might be considered a "thought disorder" or as the *DSM* calls it: *Delusions*. Ironically, this is precisely the point that Eugen Bleuler (the man who coined the term *schizophrenia*) stated about his fellow psychiatrists:

> We administer all sorts of treatments whose efficacy has never been proved, such as electricity; or treatments about which we are insufficiently informed, such as water in hydrotherapy. . . . We observe this urge to glibness among small children, among savages, among doctors, and in tales from mythology; also to some extent in the discourse of philosophers; and in morbid form, among schizophrenics, in particular. . . . It is upon this primal urge that the power of medical practice is founded.[45]

Many doctors believe these psychiatric speculations though there is no evidence to support them and much evidence to denounce them. Such a reality may very well be why Dr. Loren Mosher remarks, "Much of today's psychiatric science is based

---

[43] Thomas Szasz, *Psychiatry: The Science of Lies* (New York: Syracuse University Press, 2008), ix-x.

[44] Whitfield, *Truth about Mental Illness*, 174.

[45] Eugen Blueler, *Autistic Undisciplined Thinking in Medicine and How to Overcome it* (1911) translated by Ernest Harms (Darien, CT: Hafner Publishing, 1970), 109.

on wish, myth, and politics."[46] Beliefs maintained despite lack of evidence or contradictory evidence are referred to by the *DSM-5* as delusions — one of the major criteria for schizophrenia.[47] "False fixed beliefs" — as psychiatrists define delusions[48] — is simply another way of saying that someone is unwilling to live in reality and accept truth. With all the evidence against Kraepelin's theory, one could say that faith in the science of mental illness (and its proposed explanations for madness) is the epitome of madness itself.[49]

There is a vast difference between calling research validated truth while still attempting to provide empirical evidence and arriving at conclusive empirical evidence that reveals a natural truth (a scientific discovery). The former is hope that evidence will be discovered to validate a theory while the latter accepts whatever truth is discovered. This distinction is significant because scientists have not arrived at validated empirical evidence or biological discovery in regards to their theory of mental illness; they simply hope that their theories will someday be proved. In fact, as we will see in the chapters to come, what the natural world and God's Word both reveal is that the brain-dysfunction theory is a false belief.

In many ways, the ongoing application of the scientific process allows advocates of the brain-dysfunction theory to continue claiming validity for their theories while never having

---

[46] Peter Breggins, *Toxic Psychiatry*, back cover.

[47] APA, *DSM-5*, 87.

[48] Ibid.

[49] Thomas Szasz, *Schizophrenia: The Sacred Symbol of Psychiatry* (New York: Basic Books, 1976), 30.

scientific discovery or altering their worldview—even when evidence requires it.[50] It is the same position and practice that one must take in order to believe in evolutionary thinking. Clinical neurologist at Yale University School of Medicine, Steven Novella, explains,

> As with the study of evolution, the study of mental illness is a useful scientific paradigm. We are now venturing into a new era of increased genetic and neuroscientific understanding – progressing from the earliest phase of pure clinical description.[51]

Secularists encourage society to accept their "clinical description" or construct as fact, since evolutionists have deemed it scientific, though their theories or paradigm lack actual truth.

Understanding the Purpose of Secular Science

To make matters worse, the research on mental illness is most often conducted or funded by pharmaceutical companies who have invested interest in maintaining the brain-dysfunction theory and diligently work to ensure that scientific data is presented in their favor. Simply put, pharmaceutical companies fund research not because they are altruistic, but because there is

---

[50] Popper states, "Why, I asked, do so many scientists believe in induction? I found they did so because they believed natural science to be characterized by the inductive method—by a method starting from, and relying upon, long sequences of observations and experiments. They believed that the difference between genuine science and metaphysical or pseudo-science speculation depended solely upon whether or not the inductive method was employed. They believed (to put it in my own terminology) that only the inductive method could provide a satisfactory criterion of demarcation" (Karl Popper, *Philosophy of Science: An Historical Anthology*, 482).

[51] Steven Novella, "The Genetics of Mental Illness," http://theness.com/neurologicablog/index.php/the-genetics-of-mental-illness/.

much at stake in the business of maintaining the illusion that mental illness is biological in nature. Professor and journalist Charles Seife explains,

> In the past few years the pharmaceutical industry has come up with many ways to funnel large sums of money — enough sometimes to put a child through college — into the pockets of independent medical researchers who are doing work that bears, directly or indirectly, on the drugs these firms are making and marketing.[52]

Similarly, Dr. Abramson comments on how even highly regarded journals have endorsed the business of presenting alleged science that justifies selling medication when research shows natural remedies to be more effective:

> The purpose of this article [on the benefits of Pravachol to reduce the risk of strokes in the elderly] seemed incontrovertible" to establish "scientific evidence," legitimized by the prestige of the *New England Journal of Medicine*, that would lead doctors to believe that they were reducing their patients' risk of stroke by prescribing Pravachol. The collateral damage in establishing this belief is the diversion of doctors' and patients' attention away from far more effective ways to prevent stroke and achieve better health. But there is no profit to be made from these nondrug approaches, and therefore they receive much less attention than profitable and expensive drugs.[53]

Psychiatrist Peter Breggin likewise understands the purpose of the science being applied in mental health research:

> Implicit in all of this is the reality that organized psychiatry is big business more than it is a profession. As a big business, managed by APA and NIMH, it develops media relationships, hires PR firms, develops its medical image, holds press conferences to publicize its products, lobbies on behalf to its interests, and issues "scientific" reports that protect its members from malpractice suits by lending legitimacy to brain-damaging technologies. . . . One way to increase the overall size of the market is to convince the government, society, and individual citizens that its services are needed. From this motivation grows "official estimates" of the "prevalence of mental

---

[52] Charles Seife, "How Drug Company Money is Undermining Science," *Scientific American* 307, no. 6. (December 1, 2012).

[53] Abramson, *Overdosed America*, 17.

illness" that the media latch onto in their stories about the need for psychiatric treatment.[54]

Likewise, psychiatrist Joanna Moncrieff asserts,

> The idea that psychiatric drugs work by targeting underlying biological processes that are specific to certain sorts of mental health problems or symptoms is central to the way that psychiatric treatment is administered and presented, and to the way that research on drug treatment is designed, conducted and interpreted.[55]

Seife, Abramson, Breggin, Moncrieff, and a multitude of others recognize not only the distorted idea of science presented when pharmaceutical companies fund, conduct, and are able to interpret and publish their research, but the faith required to believe this scientism. The only remedy and safeguard against this fraud and conflict of interest, according to Seife, is to set up an accountability that protects doctors from false faith: "That way the scientific community decides whether a study is ethical and when the experiment is done, how far to trust the results."[56] In his statement, Seife identifies the two elements that are essential to every claim of scientific validity: objective research/experiments and subjective interpretations/descriptions. Psychology is no exception; consisting of (1) descriptive or objective psychology ("the experiment and research" — though this research studies the mind's effects which can be observed, and they are not truly studying the mind) and prescriptive or subjective psychology ("the scientific community decides . . . how far to trust the results"). The actual experiments and observations are one thing; the interpretations, conclusions,

---

[54] Breggin, *Toxic Psychiatry*, 366-67.

[55] Joanna Moncrieff, *The Bitterest Pills: The Troubling Story of Antipsychotic Drugs* (London: Palgrave Macmillan, 2013), 9.

[56] Seife, "Drug Company Money."

theories, and applications about an experiment are completely separate issues. The general public typically hears an interpretation of the studies or — as in the case that Dr. Abramson cites — only aspects that benefit the theory attempting to be validated. Published research almost never amounts to hard-fact without subjective interpretation involved (that is assuming that the study conducted was objective and reliable). Dr. Thomas Bodenheimer explains that the established relationship of pharmaceutical companies with researchers, peer reviews, and investigators enable big Pharma — which funds the studies they interpret — to "provide the spin on the data that favors them."[57] Subjective opinion occurs regularly in mental health research and relative and important data is often withheld by those overseeing the trials and research.[58] Since objective research provides facts that permit and even compel conclusions/interpretations to be made, the published results represent not fact, but a controlled interpretation according to a specific worldview. This reality accounts for why different interpretations of the same objective study can be made and regularly occur in other scientific fields (e.g., the fossil records in the study of origins or the "God particle" in the field of physics). Many times, though, purposeful manipulation of available facts or even withholding data is a more accurate way to describe published conclusions and psychiatric interpretations of

---

[57] Thomas Bodenheimer, "Uneasy Alliance: Clinical Investigators and the Pharmaceutical Industry," *NEJM* 342 (2000): 1539-44.

[58] D. Blumenthal et al., "Withholding Research Results by Academic Life Scientists: Evidence from a National Survey of Faculty," *JAMA* 277 (1997): 1224-28; See also P. Easterbrook et al., "Publication Bias in Clinical Research," *The Lancet* 337 (1991): 867-72.

research.[59] Former professor of psychiatry at Syracuse University, Dr. Thomas Szasz remarks,

> The widespread belief that the scientist's job is to reveal the secrets of nature is erroneous. Nature has no secrets; only persons do. Secrecy implies agency, absent in nature . . . . The human sciences are not merely unlike the physical sciences; they are, in many ways, opposites. Whereas nature neither lies nor tells the truth, persons habitually do both. This is why deception is a useful tool for person such as detectives whose job is to ferret out other people's secrets; why deception is a useful tool also for so-called experts—such as psychiatrists, psychologists, and politicians—whose ostensible job is to explain and predict certain human behaviors, especially behaviors some people consider dangerous or undesirable; and why such experts habitually deceive others and themselves.[60]

Since human nature is deceived above all other things, it makes sense that in order to explain the human condition, people would choose to utilize the tool which is most familiar to them. But deception does not free mankind from his greatest problems; truth does.

Other times, it is not manipulation or wrong interpretation of research that is misleading but merely applying ongoing research that enables a façade of science when the natural world or other studies have repeatedly disproved theory. The more research that is done the more a hypothesis appears to be scientifically sound—even if this practice means that research be terminated midway through if the discoveries appear to disprove current theories or the financial backer's intended purpose.[61] While the evidence discovered is inconclusive and

---

[59] K. Dickersin, "The Existence of Publication Bias and Risk Factors for Its Occurrence," *JAMA* 263 (1990): 1385-89; See also John Abramson, *Overdosed America: The Broken Promise of American Medicine* (New York: HarperCollins, 2005), and I. Chalmers, "Underreporting Research Is Scientific Misconduct," *JAMA* 263 (1990): 405-8.

[60] Szasz, *Psychiatry: The Science of Lies*, ix.

[61] Abramson, *Overdosed America*, 104-5.

sometimes even contrary to the original hypothesis, secularists still claim that they are close to discovering and realizing their desired results. Such a practice enables them to maintain the perception that their theory is both reliable and valid.

One example of this unscientific process is found in the psychiatric theory of bipolar disorder. One of the secular authorities on the subject, Dr. Francis Mondimore, writes,

> Despite literally hundreds of years examining the bodily fluids and brain tissues of individual with mood disorders—first with the naked eye, then with microscopes, later with x-rays and scanning devices, and more recently with incredibly sophisticated biochemical probes—no one has been able to find in patients with this illness [bipolar] any abnormalities that can be accurately and reliably measured as an aid in diagnosing the disorder. Although work in the genetics of bipolar disorder holds the promise that genetic markers for the illness may be discovered in the not-too-distant future—suggesting that a blood test might be possible that will identify at least some cases of the illness. . . . The clinical applications of these findings are still in the future.[62]

In the meantime, even before any scientific validation occurs, theories morph into dogma which society accepts in confidence. It is commonly believed that bipolar disorder is genetically or chemically caused, yet no objective evidence exists to verify these theories even after endless research has been conducted.[63]

To complicate matters, what researchers often suggest to be empirical evidence are correlations rather than empirical findings. For example, in the case of those labeled as bipolar, research seems to indicate that physical illnesses are associated with the specific mindsets and behaviors. This correlation does not validate bipolar as an illness as the NIMH rightly explains:

---

[62] Francis Mark Mondimore, *Bipolar Disorder: A Guide for Patients and Families*, 3rd ed. (Baltimore: Johns Hopkins University Press, 2014), 29.

[63] Whitfield, *Truth about Mental Illness*, 38. See also Breggin, *Toxic Psychiatry*, 135-37.

> People with bipolar disorder are at higher risk for thyroid disease, migraine headaches, heart disease, diabetes, obesity, and other physical illnesses. These illnesses may cause symptoms of mania or depression, or they may be caused by some medications used to treat bipolar disorder.[64]

Though they admit these correlations are indecisive, they are unwilling to concede other dogmatic claims as also being correlations and not empirical evidence. Proving cause and effect in the mind-brain connection is not always possible through scientific means. This is precisely the point that Dr. Breggin makes about many of his fellow psychiatrists' claims that depression and bipolar disorders are caused by fluctuating chemical levels in the brain. He states, "The fact that biochemical changes take place in the brain in association with intense moods proves nothing about which comes first."[65] Effects can be confused with causes and causes with effects. Often studies which are conducted with proper controls provide new insight, yet the professional is left to determine or to interpret the results. Another example is found in the brains of those who are labeled as having bipolar disorder. MRI studies have found that the prefrontal cortex of the brain in those labeled as bipolar tends to be smaller than people considered to be "normal."[66] Is this physical change caused by wrong or sinful mindsets and behaviors (such as pride, self-absorption, and immorality as identified in the *DSM*), stressful or hurtful life events, lack of

---

[64] "What is Bipolar Disorder?" http://www.nimh.nih.gov/health/publications/bipolar-disorder-in-adults/index.shtml.

[65] Breggin, *Toxic Psychiatry*, 144.

[66] Francis Mark Mondimore, *Bipolar Disorder: A Guide for Patients and Families*, 3rd ed. (Baltimore: Johns Hopkins University Press, 2014), 29. See also "What is Bipolar Disorder?" available from http://www.nimh.nih.gov/health/publications/bipolar-disorder-in-adults/index.shtml.

sleep, or are the behaviors caused by these physical differences? Many secularists interpret the smaller brains and structural difference of those labeled as bipolar as potential proof that bipolar disorder is legitimate and caused by brain-dysfunction:

> This structure and its connections to other parts of the brain mature during adolescence, *suggesting* that abnormal development of this brain circuit *may account* for why the disorder tends to emerge during a person's teen years [emphasis added].[67]

The use of the words *suggesting* and *may* indicates that the study is inconclusive and the NIMH's statement is simply one interpretation of data. Yet the unproven theory is believed to be true, promoted as dogma, and claimed as solid support for the existence and origins of bipolar disorder.[68]

In the case of bipolar, ADHD and most other claimed psychiatric disorders, no scientific research or data exists to prove that these psychiatric labels are valid ideas let alone medical issues caused by genetics, chemical imbalances, or brain malfunctions.[69] In fact, Dr. Whitfield notes this truth across all the constructs of mental illness:

> In late 2003 a group of Ph.D. and M.D. clinicians and researchers challenge the American Psychiatric Association to identify one published study that proved the biogenetic theory of mental illness. The APA was unable to do so.[70]

He goes on to explain,

---

[67] "What is Bipolar Disorder?" http://www.nimh.nih.gov/health/publications/bipolar-disorder-in-adults/index.shtml.

[68] Whitfield, *Truth About Mental Illness*, 265.

[69] Breggin, *Toxic Psychiatry*, 183.

[70] Whitfield, *Truth about Mental Illness*, 256.

Clinical and research psychologist Jay Joseph has extensively reviewed the genetic studies on psychiatric illness that have been reported over the last century. After reanalyzing this large body of reports that favored a genetic origin for most mental illnesses, he concluded that this research is greatly flawed and that its conclusions are mostly invalid. As an example, he notes that the various methods used to look for possible genetic transmission are either invalid or methodologically flawed.[71]

Even the NIMH admits in regard to the etiology of bipolar disorder that

Scientists are studying the *possible causes* of bipolar disorder. Most agree that there is no single cause. Rather, many factors *likely* [emphasis.added] act together to produce the illness or increase risk for developing it.[72]

To state it differently, scientists — mostly funded by pharmaceutical companies — are taking secularists' ideas of "possible causes," suggesting that they are true, and then trying to validate these theories. Unfortunately for secular researchers and the pharmaceutical companies that fund them, no one will ever see evidence to validate the theories of materialism or determinism on which the construct of mental illness rests. Yet, these theories are growingly believed to be true and believed to be scientific.

Obtaining empirical evidence or findings that can be manipulated or interpreted enough to pass as evidence has become one of the most important commodities of pharmaceutical companies and the reason they fund so much research on mental illness:

It's not news that medical research has become big business, often with billions of dollars on the line. The problem is that the search for scientific truth is, by its very nature, unpredictable, and this uncertainty is hardly optimal from a business point of view. There is far too much at stake to leave this process to the uncertainties of science. In this context, the role of the drug and medical-device

---

[71] Ibid., 257.

[72] "What is Bipolar Disorder?" http://www.nimh.nih.gov/health/.

companies has evolved so that their most important products are no longer the things they make. Now their most important product is "scientific evidence." This is what drives sales. In this commercial context, the age-old standards of good science are being quietly but radically weakened, and in some cases abandoned.[73]

The science and medicine of mental illness are not healing arts or objective approaches; they instead represent a corrupt and agenda-driven business of creating empirical evidence. The renowned journal the *Lancet* explains in an editorial written in 2002:

The escalating influence of big pharma in medicine persuaded editors of medical journals to come together last year and agree strict rules on reporting sponsorship and conflicts of interest (see *Lancet* 2001; 358: 854–56). While this consensus sets the highest standards yet for disclosing commercial influences in medical research, there are signs that it does not go far enough—or, at the very least, that this guidance is not being fully heeded. A study of the interactions between authors of clinical practice guidelines and the pharmaceutical industry, published in *JAMA* in February, found serious omissions in declarations of conflicts of interest. Almost 90% of authors received research funding from or acted as consultants for a drug company. Over half had connections with companies whose drugs were being reviewed in the guideline, and the same proportion indicated that there was no formal procedure for reporting these interactions. The guidelines studied covered all fields where prescription drug use has seen the greatest increases.[74]

We observed this unethical conflict of interest in volume 1,[75] but this entry in the prestigious *Lancet* reveals that the majority of research being conducted and presented as scientific and medically sound is questionable to say the least. We also saw that deception is found throughout the research on mental health and is usually funded by the pharmaceutical companies,

---

[73] John Abramson, *Overdosed America: The Broken Promise of American Medicine* (New York: HarperCollins, 2005), 94.

[74] "Just How Tainted Has Medicine Become?" editorial, *The Lancet* 359, no. 9313 (April 6, 2002): 1167.

[75] Daniel R. Berger II, *Mental Illness: The Necessity for Faith and Authority* (Taylors, SC: Alethia International Publishers, 2016), 103-9.

yet these studies usually have great influence over people's beliefs about what is true concerning their mind-brain connection. The bottom line is that claims are often falsified or purposely distorted by pharmaceutical companies and the psychiatrists they pay in order to attempt validation of subjective theories, and the marketing of such science results in many people accepting such fraud as fact. Psychiatrist Peter Breggin notes,

> In the world of modern psychiatry, claims can become truth, hopes can become achievements, and propaganda is taken as science. Nowhere is this more obvious than in psychiatric pretensions concerning the genetics, biology, and physical treatment of depression and mania (bipolar). As we also found in regard to neuroleptics and so-called schizophrenia, biopsychiatric research is based too often on distortions, incomplete information, and sometimes outright fraud—at the expense of reason and science.[76]

Likewise, Dr. Charles Whitfield writes,

> The required FDA-controlled clinical trials for their drugs' efficacy tend to be not only too short in duration (e.g., from only five to eight weeks), but the drug companies and their paid researchers/authors often manipulate the study design or research methods and their reporting to make their drugs look more successful. These distortions often end up providing the public and their clinicians with misinformation about both the disorders and the drugs.[77]

Dr. Ray Williams also explains,

> Looking further, it's evident that the pharmaceutical industry is fraught with fraud. For instance, the new generation of antipsychotics is the single biggest target of the False Claims Act. Every major drug company selling the drugs has either settled recent

---

[76] Breggin, *Toxic Psychiatry*, 182-83.

[77] Charles Whitfield, *Truth about Mental Illness, The Truth about Mental Illness: Choices for Healing* (Deerfield Beach, FL: Health Communications, 2004), 217.

government cases for hundreds of millions of dollars or is under investigation for health care fraud.[78]

Similarly, nationwide studies that yield vital information concerning psychotropic drugs have often been hidden from public knowledge—such as the evidence against the efficacy of antidepressants noted in the *New England Journal of Medicine*.[79] Breggin comments on another similar study,

> The federal government sponsored a highly publicized nationwide study of the effects on the brain of taking multiple street drugs, such as narcotics and hallucinogens. A serendipitous finding came up in the mental patient control group: the consumption of neuroleptic drugs was directly associated with a permanent loss of overall mental function. If the drug had been marijuana, or even tobacco or alcohol, the results of this authoritative study would have been instantly flashed across the nation by media. Not so when the brains of mental patients are balanced against the reputations of psychiatrists. The reputations nearly always carry the day.[80]

Dr. Abramson also remarks on the alleged scientific evidence for anxiety and depression disorders,

> The drug companies have a great deal at stake in persuading doctors and the public to limit their view of social anxiety disorder and depression to the biomedical model of disease. They provide persuasive "scientific" explanations for mental health symptoms, while deflecting consideration of the evidence that, in many cases, lifestyle changes and short-term counseling offer more enduring benefit. Not coincidentally, their approach is also the best way to sell more drugs.[81]

---

[78] Ray B. Williams, "How Drug Companies Are Undermining Scientific Research," http://www.psychologytoday.com/blog/wired-success/201212/how-drug-companies-are-undermining-scientific-research.

[79] Erick H. Turner, Annette M. Matthews, Eftihia Linardatos, Robert A. Tell, and Robert Rosenthal, "Selective Publication of Antidepressant Trials and Its Influence on Apparent Efficacy," *New England Journal of Medicine* 358 (January 17, 2008): 252-60.

[80] Peter Breggin, *Toxic Psychiatry*, 82.

[81] Abramson, *Overdosed America*, 234.

So-called scientific research and the published results revealed to the general public are not always the whole picture or even an accurate one.[82] Studies consistently reveal that research which favors pharmaceutical companies' agendas are commonly published, whereas objective studies that reveal psychotropic drugs to lack efficacy or show clear dangers of specific drugs are consistently withheld from publication:

> Regarding pharmacological interventions, cases of reporting bias were, for example, identified in the treatment of the following conditions: depression, bipolar disorder, schizophrenia, anxiety disorder, attention-deficit hyperactivity disorder.... Many cases involved the withholding of study data by manufacturers and regulatory agencies or the active attempt by manufacturers to suppress publication. The ascertained effects of reporting bias included the overestimation of efficacy and the underestimation of safety risks of interventions.[83]

The corruption is so bad that in 2001, twelve of the most highly regarded medical journals — including the *NEJM, JAMA,* and the *Lancet* — issued a joint statement that warned that pharmaceutical companies were manipulating research and data to meet their needs and desires. Conclusions were then drawn from these studies and articles written and published in various respected journals. Dr. Abramson comments on this shocking reality:

> In words that should have shaken the medical profession to its core, the statement told of "draconian" terms being imposed on medical researchers by corporate sponsors. And it warned that the "precious objectivity" of the clinical studies that were being published in their journals was being threatened by the transformation of clinical research into a commercial activity. The editors said that the use of commercially sponsored clinical trials "primarily for marketing . . . makes a mockery of clinical investigation and is a misuse of a

---

[82] Ibid., 96-97.

[83] Natalie McGauran et al., "Reporting Bias in Medical Research - a Narrative Review," *Trials* 11 (2010): 37. See also John Abramson, *Overdosed America: The Broken Promise of American Medicine* (New York: HarperCollins, 2005), 23-38.

powerful tool." Medical scientists working on corporate-sponsored research the editors warned "may have little or no input into trial design, no access to the raw data, and limited participation in data interpretation."[84]

The sobering truth is simple: belief in the science of mental illness is equivalent to blind faith in big Pharma marketing disguised as objective science.

Because of this reality, pharmaceutical companies may possess even more authority than do the APA or FDA. In fact, psychiatrist Thomas Szasz notes that the mechanism enabling the wide acceptance of mental illness is really political control and not actually the science that psychiatrists claim:

> There is confusion—in the minds of these experts, in their accounts, and in psychiatry generally—about the differences between science and politics, between medical diagnosis as technical taxonomy and psychiatric diagnosis as political action. Scientific propositions are supported by evidence: for example, the proposition that paresis is a syphilitic infection of the brain is buttressed by the evidence of *Treponema pallid* in the brains of such patients. Political actions, on the other hand, are supported not by evidence but by power: for example, the policy of forcibly confining certain people without accusing them of a crime or trying them for it, and forcibly imposing the stigmatizing label "schizophrenia" on them, is buttressed not by any evidence of morphological lesions in their brain, but by the power of the authorities to act in these particular ways toward these particular persons. . . . For example, when the Nazis stigmatize and segregate Jews, that is persecution; when the Americans stigmatize and segregate their fellow Americans who have black skin or Japanese ancestry, that is also persecution. But when people throughout the world stigmatize and segregate their relatives and neighbors who behave in ways which the majority do not like—and when that stigmatization is carried out by means of pseudomedical stigmata and pseudomedical segregations—then it is generally accepted not as persecution, but psychiatry.[85]

Psychiatry is not a science but a mechanism of social control. Many professionals even believe that the APA, NIMH, big Pharma, and the FDA are too closely related, and they rightly

---

[84] Abramson, *Overdosed America*, 96.

[85] Thomas Szasz, *Schizophrenia: The Sacred Symbol of Psychiatry* (New York: Basic Books, 1976), 108.

note how these inappropriate relationships have eliminated checks and balances and enabled social control. In making his own case, psychopharmacologist Fred Leavitt quotes Peter Schrag:

> Most of the major figures in drug research serve as consultants to drug firms and, at the same time, to the [NIMH] and the Food and Drug Administration, which licenses the drugs. They review each other's grant proposals sit on the same committees work on the same studies, write for each other's journals. NIMH employees collaborate with drug-company consultants in mental health research; NIMH consultants appear before FDA review committees on behalf of drug companies; editors of journals heavily supported by drug-company advertising serve on "impartial" FDA committees reviewing the safety and efficacy of medication produced by their advertisers.[86]

Similarly, Dr. Abramson explains,

> Completely invisible to the public, officials at the National Institutes of Health are allowed to participate in lucrative consulting contracts with the drug companies. Experts with financial ties to the drug companies dominate the FDA's Advisory Committees and the panels that write the clinical guidelines that define the standards of care for practicing doctors. The medical industry even funds the majority of doctors' continuing education.[87]

Such practices have led many professionals to admit that[88] "the [drug] industry's ubiquitous influence has corrupted the integrity of medical research and the scientific literature upon which scientific research is built."[89] It is no wonder that many

---

[86] Fred Leavitt, *Drugs and Behavior* (London: Sage Publications, 1995), 272; taken from Peter Schrag, *Mind Control* (New York: Pantheon, 1978).

[87] Abramson, *Overdosed America*, 234.

[88] For further study, see Peter Breggin, *Toxic Psychiatry*, 344-70.

[89] "Just How Tainted Has Medicine Become?" editorial, *The Lancet* 359, no. 9313 (April 6, 2002): 1167.

psychiatrists feel that "deception and coercion are intrinsic to the practices of the mental health profession."[90]

Not only are facts denied or distorted, but medical articles are regularly published in respected journals such as *JAMA* and *NEJM* that directly contradict FDA findings without consequence or correction.[91] When physicians and journalists read these published lies in such respected medical journals, the belief is perpetuated in spite of the facts.[92]

One must ignore or deny the overwhelming deception, fraud, and bias that exist in the relationship between the American Psychiatric Association, the pharmaceutical companies, and their evolutionary approach to the natural world in order to accept the ideology that medication helps those with mental and behavioral struggles. In fact, there exists overwhelming evidence produced by third party researchers that psychotropic medications hurt individuals and society more than they have ever helped.[93] Yet beliefs marketed as "science"

---

[90] Szasz, *Psychiatry: The Science of Lies*, 1.

[91] Abramson, *Overdosed America*, 23-38.

[92] Furthermore, many pharmaceutical companies falsify the high costs of research, and then charge the consumer for this exaggeration. See Ray B. Williams, "How Drug Companies Are Undermining Scientific Research," http://www.psychologytoday.com/blog/wired-success/201212/how-drug-companies-are-undermining-scientific-research. See also, Charles L. Whitfield, *The Truth about Mental Illness: Choices for Healing* (Deerfield Beach, FL: Health Communications, 2004), 226.

[93] For further reading on this subject, see Stuart Kirk, Tomi Gomory, and David Cohen, *Mad Science: Psychiatric Coercion, Diagnosis, and Drugs* (New Brunswick, NJ: Transaction Publishers, 2013); Peter Breggin, *Medication Madness: The Role of Psychiatric Drugs in Cases of Violence, Suicide and Murder* (St. Martin's

within the construct of mental illness have convinced many that mental turmoil and impairment equals biological illness.

Defining Descriptive and Prescriptive Psychology

It is also important that we delineate the differences between descriptive (objective) and prescriptive (subjective) psychology. Even in Freud's day, such distinctions were made within secular science:

> In the German culture within which Freud lived, and which permeated his work, there existed and still exists a definite and important division between two approaches to knowledge. Both disciplines are called *Wissenshaften* (sciences; literally knowledge), and they are accepted as equal in their approaches to their fields, although their methods have hardly anything in common. These two are the *Naturwissenschaften* (natural sciences) and, opposed to them in content and in methods, the *Geisteswissenschaften*. The term *Geisteswissenschaften* defies translation into English; its literal meaning is "sciences of the spirit," and the concept is one that is deeply rooted in German idealist philosophy.[94]

This reality plays out in modern day scientific fields and psychology as well with descriptive psychology representing natural sciences and prescriptive psychology representing philosophy and theory. The evolutionary geneticist Richard Lewontin explains,

> Science serves two functions. First, it provides us with new ways of manipulating the material world by producing a set of techniques, practices, and inventions by which new things are produced and by which the quality of our lives is changed.... The second function of science, which is sometimes independent and sometimes closely related to the first, is the function of explanation. Even if scientists are not actually changing the material mode of our existence, they are constantly explaining why things are the way they are. It is often said that these *theories about the world* [what secularists call science]

Press, 2008); or John Abramson, *Overdosed America: The Broken Promise of American Medicine* (New York: HarperCollins, 2005).

[94] Bruno Bettelheim, *Freud and Man's Soul: An Important Re-Interpretation of Freudian Theory* (New York: Vintage Books, 1983), 40-41.

must be produced in order, ultimately, to change the world through practice [emphasis added].[95]

Though the scientific method and the research it produces are necessary as we attempt to make sense of the natural world, not all theories derived from them are valid. Theory should not be considered to be of equal importance as objective fact, nor should experiments and interpretations be presented as inseparable or one in the same. However, because all experiments must be interpreted, all published research that presents a conclusion contains some level of inescapable subjectivity.

Descriptive Psychology

Whereas prescriptive psychology is theory and reflects one's worldview, descriptive psychology is an attempt to objectively study the natural world. We must reiterate though, that the scientist's moral nature cannot ever be detached from his involvement in the natural world. Descriptive psychology can be a legitimate pursuit, but we have seen that much fraud and bias exist in mental illness research:[96]

> Scientists who conduct the research are too often being unduly influenced by the drug industry, as are some bioethicists (who are supposed to watch and help them to be honest). This escalating and precarious situation is similar to the fox guarding the hen house. Finally, many otherwise reputable professional associations, such as the American Psychiatric Association, are increasingly funded by drug companies, and thereby are possibly losing their objectivity.[97]

---

[95] Richard Lewontin, *Biology as Ideology: The Doctrine of DNA* (New York: HarperCollins, 1991), 4.

[96] Natalie McGauran et al., "Reporting Bias in Medical Research: A Narrative Review," *Trials* 11 (2010): 37.

[97] Whitfield, *Truth about Mental Illness,* 220.

Truly ethical scientists, however, will do all they can to make their studies objective and seek to discover or better understand the existing truth in the natural world. They will accept the conclusions even if it means they reject their beloved but invalidated theory and shift their paradigm. Descriptive psychology focuses on experiments, testing, and research, and in theory it seeks to discover or further study existing truths. Controlled studies can be reliable and, if validated, can be used to further understand special and natural revelation (e.g., the ant can be studied to better understand the character qualities that Proverbs 6:6 discusses). However valuable scientific research might be, it is important for us to understand that God's supernatural truth as revealed in Scripture is never dependent upon the natural world He created or alleged scientific discovery.[98] Discovered truth in the natural world certainly can increase understanding and application, but it is not necessary to have faith in God. If scientific conclusions are truth, however, discoveries will agree with Scripture, since both natural revelation and special revelation are both God's gifts to mankind and are in complete harmony.

We must also reiterate that psychological research is not truly studying the mind as the word *psychology* asserts. What researchers observe are outworking behaviors of the mind and the brain. Calling psychology science, then, is actually a miscategorization, since science cannot study the mind. Science can, however study human responses, actions, influences, physical effects, and patterns — anything that is observable.

Additionally, as we will see in later chapters, experimental psychology can offer clarity and testimony of God's revelation.

---

[98] Jay E. Adams, *How to Help People Change: The Four-Step Biblical Process* (Grand Rapids: Zondervan, 1986), 34, 36.

42

We are not after proof that God's Word is true by means of descriptive psychology, since we have accepted that reality by faith. Descriptive psychology, then, can be helpful, but it is not necessary to approach the human mind, its struggles, or its produced behavior.

Prescriptive Psychology

Every new discovery or further understanding realized ignites within us the universal human urge to explain and categorize these findings according to a certain worldview. Truth is not of great value to us personally or corporately unless it can be practically applied. This practice of conforming objective truth or descriptive psychology into theory is prescriptive psychology. In other words, our physical observations of the natural world become valuable to us when they are interpreted through our philosophical perspective. The physical and spiritual natures are not to be compartmentalized and neither are our spiritual and physical realities. In fact, the Bible establishes that God not only made the physical realm from his spiritual nature (Proverbs 3:19; Hebrews 11:1-3), but He also made the physical world to reveal the spiritual realm. David says in Psalm 104:24, "O LORD, how manifold are your works! In wisdom have you made them all; the earth is full of your creatures."[99] Likewise, Proverbs 3:19 connects God's wisdom and God's creation, and Proverbs 6:6-11 expresses the idea that parental teaching of a spiritual/moral lesson can often be best taught by using the physical world. In theology, these ideas are referred to as natural revelation and special revelation, but they are always interrelated. In the New Testament, Jesus used parables (illustrations of natural revelation) to teach divine

---

[99] The *ESV* is used throughout this book unless otherwise noted.

truths about Himself and mankind (e.g., Matthew 13; seeds, weeds, treasures, and nets . . .). Scripture reveals throughout that the physical world is to be understood by faith as it is interpreted through the lens of Scripture. The order of the physical world reflects the order of the metaphysical world, and they are both matters of faith. Marginalizing or denying the Scriptural perspective, then, erodes the foundation necessary for solid scientific progress.

Accordingly, everyone has a choice to make on how they will perceive and explain the human physical nature. People can either trust in humanity's own erring thoughts, or they can depend upon God's wisdom to interpret the natural world and practically guide their decisions. But God insists that the beginning of true wisdom is to fear Him rather than to trust in one's own way and ideas (Proverbs 1:7; 3:5-6).

Psychological and psychiatric theories — which have no empirical support though they are thoroughly researched — represent prescriptive/subjective psychology. We can look at behaviors, mindsets, and personalities objectively, but we all by nature must interpret this information from our worldview/ faith. When someone from the scientific community speaks or writes, it is important and helpful to understand and discern which type of psychology (descriptive or prescriptive) is being applied. When reading journals and suggested correlations in research, we should learn to recognize words and phrases such as "seems to indicate," "suggests," "potential," "likely," "most clinicians/professionals agree" as indicating theory or hypothesis (subjective psychology) rather than objective fact. We must also think through other possible explanations that might better explain correlations or alleged claims.

For the Christian, any worldview which perceives the natural world to glorify mankind instead of the one true Creator must be rejected. Romans 1:22-25 states,

> Claiming to be wise, they became fools, and exchanged the glory of the immortal God for images resembling mortal man and birds and animals and creeping things. Therefore God gave them up in the lusts of their hearts to impurity, to the dishonoring of their bodies among themselves, because they exchanged the truth about God for a lie and worshiped and served the creature rather than the Creator, who is blessed forever! Amen.

It is not mere coincidence that when humanism and materialism gained acceptance in America, destructive behavior — even as described in psychiatric constructs of mental illness — also increased. Some Christians seemingly reject the humanistic philosophy and Darwinian thinking while still arguing that believers should buy into the idea of secular science and can use the "scientific" classification system laid out in the *DSM* (*Diagnostic and Statistical Manual*).[100] Yet, as was discussed, this entire system was created as the practical outworking of rejecting God as the authority over the immaterial mind — a way to keep God out of remedying the mind. Passages in Scripture, such as 2 Corinthians 10:4-5 forbid this type of thinking for believers:

> For the weapons of our warfare are not of the flesh but have divine power to destroy strongholds. We destroy arguments and every lofty opinion raised against the knowledge of God, and take every thought captive to obey Christ.

This text sets forth two relevant truths and responsibilities for the believer: (1) to reject all human speculation and arguments that oppose God's wisdom, and (2) to control our naturally unrestrained thoughts and ideas. Both of these ideas center on

---

[100] American Psychiatric Association, *Diagnostic and Statistical Manual of Mental Disorders: DSM-5* (Washington, D.C.: American Psychiatric Association, 2013). Hereafter referred to as *DSM*.

the importance of the true knowledge of God. To disobey either of these instructions (to control our thoughts and dismantle warped ideas) is to disregard our desperate mental state, to encourage wrong thinking, and to reject hope for transformation and healing.

Certainly, the secular construct of mental illness was created because God's revelation was rejected. Integrating evolutionary ideas with God's revelation cannot logically or practically occur without detrimental results. Likewise, claiming that the APA's system found in the *DSM* is useful helps to establish the APA as the authority over mindsets, emotions, and behavior and brings into question God's detailed descriptions of and remedy for the human psyche.

Confusing the Two

Confusing descriptive and prescriptive psychology have led many people to believe the false claims of secular science. Many times so-called new findings in the mental health field are dogmatically presented and marketed to the general public, which accepts them blindly. For example, scientific tests are conducted (descriptive psychology), and conclusions or interpretations are formed and published (prescriptive psychology). Consumers are told that a theory is scientifically sound, and society in general accepts the theory without hesitation. Americans have been conditioned not to question science as it is assumed to be reliable and valid. When research is published, the actual study and the interpretation seem to be one in the same. The reader is left thinking that to deny the unproven theory presented in a medical or scientific journal is to deny the research as well. But this is simply not the case. Ignorance and confusion of the two types of psychology regularly enable conjecture to flourish as fact.

One of the most prominent examples is that of alleged chemical imbalances that are regularly claimed to cause many mental illnesses. Most people believe that this idea is scientifically supported and thus it is objective, when in fact it is only a well marketed but speculative theory.[101] Noted authority on psychosurgery, neuroscientist Elliot Valenstein, explains his own findings:

> It may surprise you to learn that there is no convincing evidence that most mental patients have any chemical imbalance. Yet many physicians tell their patients that they are suffering from a chemical imbalance, despite the reality that there are no tests available for assessing the chemical status of a living person's brain. While there are some reports of finding evidence of an excess or deficiency in the activity of a particular neurotransmitter system in the brains of deceased mental patients, these claims are controversial, as other investigators cannot find any such relationship.[102]

Similarly, psychiatrist Joanna Moncrieff states,

> It is important to realize at the start that no chemical imbalance or other biological process that might explain drug action in a disease-centered way has been substantiated for any psychiatric disorder. The serotonin theory of depression and the dopamine hypothesis of schizophrenia, which appear to suggest that drugs act in this way, remain merely hypotheses. Most authorities now admit that there is no evidence that depression is associated with abnormalities of serotonin or noradrenaline, as used to be believed. There is also little empirical support for the dopamine hypothesis of schizophrenia . . . and many psychiatric researchers acknowledge it is at least inadequate as an explanation for the aetiology of schizophrenia. The fact that the theory will not die, despite decades of contradictory findings, illustrated the importance of portraying the action of antipsychotics in disease-centered terms.[103]

Dr. Robert Whitaker also remarks,

> The low-serotonin hypothesis of depression and the high-dopamine hypothesis of schizophrenia had always been the twin pillars of the chemical-imbalance theory of mental disorders, and by the late

---

[101] Whitfield, *Truth about Mental Illness*, 38.

[102] Elliot Valenstein, *Blaming the Brain: the Truth about Drugs and Mental Health* (New York: Basic Books, 1998), 4.

[103] Moncrieff, *The Bitterest Pills*, 7.

1980s, both had been found wanting. Other mental disorders have also been touted to the public as diseases caused by chemical imbalances, but there was never any evidence to support those claims.[104]

Professor of Medicine at Harvard University, Irving Kirsch, also notes this reality:

> The conventional view of depression is that it is caused by chemical imbalance in the brain. . . . I examine the chemical-imbalance theory. You may be surprised to learn that it is actually a rather controversial theory and that there is not much scientific evidence to support it. While writing this chapter I came to an even stronger conclusion. It is not just that there is not much supportive evidence; rather, there is a ton of data indicating that the chemical-imbalance theory is simply wrong.[105]

Though many secularists still assert that chemical imbalance is a valid and scientific etiology for mental disorders, the lack of empirical evidence and the complexity of the brain reveal this theory to be merely an unproven hypothesis and not descriptive or objective psychology at all. Secular psychiatrist and psychopharmacologist David Healy writes about the etiology of alleged chemical imbalances:

> Most patients are told this but it is completely wrong. We have no idea about which interplay of psychosocial conditions, biochemical processes, receptors and neural pathways that lead to mental disorders and the theories that patients with depression lack serotonin and that patients with schizophrenia have too much dopamine have long been refuted. The truth is just the opposite. There is no chemical imbalance to begin with, but when treating mental illness with drugs, we create a chemical imbalance, an artificial condition that the brain tries to counteract.[106]

---

[104] Robert Whitaker, *Anatomy of an Epidemic: Magic Bullets, Psychiatric Drugs, and the Astonishing Rise of Mental Illness in America* (New York: Broadway Books, 2015), 77.

[105] Irving Kirsch, *The Emperor's New Drugs: Exploding the Antidepressant Myth* (New York: Basic Books, 2011), preface 5-6.

[106] David Healy, "Psychiatry Gone Astray," http://davidhealy.org/psychiatry-gone-astray/.

In short, secularists imply a non-existent normal standard of chemical levels in the brain (i.e., "chemical imbalances," specifically in the neurotransmitters) as a potential cause of many mental illnesses. However, chemical levels not only differ between individuals, rendering a standard level of each brain chemical impossible across a defined social spectrum, but chemicals also fluctuate at high levels in each individual (between different emotions, activities, and mental processes) and make so-called normal levels of brain chemicals immeasurable.[107] These differences make the determination of a set standard of normal chemical balance impossible and in turn invalidate the etiological claim of chemical imbalances to explain mental illness. David Burns of Stanford University stresses this point:

> We cannot measure brain serotonin levels in living human beings, so there is no way to test this theory. Some neuroscientists would question whether the theory of chemical imbalance is even viable, since the brain does not function in this way, as a hydraulic system.[108]

Psychiatrist Peter Breggin also comments,

> Meanwhile, no causal relationship has ever been established between a specific biochemical state of the brain and any specific behavior, and it is simplistic to assume it is possible. What we do know is that some changes can increase the likelihood of one kind of activity or another but only in the most general fashion, usually based on the individual's preexisting attitudes.[109]

---

[107] John Rosemond and Bose Ravenel, *The Diseasing of America's Children: Exposing the ADHD Fiasco and Empowering Parents to Take Back Control* (Nashville: Thomas Nelson, 2008), 64-65.

[108] David Burns as quoted by Melody Petersen, *Our Daily Meds* (New York: Sarah Crichton Books, 2008), 105.

[109] Breggin, *Toxic Psychiatry*, 142.

He goes on to comment about alleged chemical imbalances in those diagnosed as depressed,

> Some drugs are used to treat depression on the theory that they enhance serotonergic neurotransmission; but in reality they cause extreme imbalances in the system, including a relative compensatory shutdown of serotonergic neurotransmission. . . . Since the brain typically tries to compensate for any artificially induced biochemical imbalance, drugs are too likely to achieve the opposite of what we intend. We cannot at present scientifically confirm the suggested relationship between sluggish serotonergic neurotransmission and some destructive or self-destructive behaviors. Meanwhile, there is even less evidence that people routinely diagnosed as depressed by psychiatrists have biochemical imbalances. Scientific reviews of the biochemistry of depression have failed to identify a consistent biochemical basis.[110]

Not only can doctors and scientists not know when a chemical is imbalanced, but attempts to balance that which is unknown regularly causes damage to the brain and nervous system. In spite of this reality, such theories are widely marketed by secularists and readily accepted by society. Unlike valid physical changes that can occur in the brain, chemical imbalance is merely an unproven subjective theory that makes psychotropic drugs seem like the best viable option to remedy (or help in coping) people's mental problems. In fact, the chemical imbalance theory is in large part the main argument for using neuroleptics to treat the mind's problems. Psychiatrist Joanna Moncrieff explains,

> This expansion in the use of antipsychotic drugs has been dependent on a theoretical framework that casts psychiatric drugs as specifically targeted treatments that work by reversing or ameliorating an underlying brain abnormality or dysfunction. The nature of the abnormality is often referred to as a "chemical imbalance," and drug company websites repeatedly stress the idea

---

[110] Ibid., 142-43.

that psychiatric medication works by rectifying a chemical imbalance.[111]

She later writes,

> By helping to establish the idea that antipsychotics exert a disease-specific action in schizophrenia and psychosis as unquestioned fact, the dopamine hypothesis [chemical imbalance] has helped to create the impression that antipsychotics might have disease-specific actions in the many other circumstances in which they are now employed.[112]

Without validating the speculative theory of chemical imbalances, psychiatric medications amount to merely chemical restraints.

Too often what is marketed and sold as objective findings and validated fact in the "scientific field" of mental health is in fact only prescriptive psychology based on faith in secular presuppositions. What we as believers must do is to take everything to the Scriptures to first discern God's view before believing the latest and greatest scientific find. Natural revelation will never contradict God's special revelation found in His Word. God's Word, not medicine or science, is the best source available to understand the immaterial mind. However, whichever worldview one chooses to believe in approaching the mind and human behavior — either secular science or God's wisdom, it is first and foremost a decision of faith.

---

[111] Joanna Moncrieff, *The Bitterest Pills: The Troubling Story of Antipsychotic Drugs* (London: Palgrave Macmillan, 2013), 7.

[112] Ibid., 12.

CHAPTER 2 – THE LIMITATIONS OF NEUROIMAGING

What differentiates something from being a matter of faith to being physical matter—able to be observed and the scientific process applied—is the human ability to see, touch, or engage the other senses in studies versus having to spiritually discern or to see a reality without the benefit of our physical senses. Beliefs can be false, but as we established in the first chapter, so too can the necessary physical perceptions and conclusions about sensory realities. In fact, they can be outright wrong. While many professionals champion the technologies of neuroimaging as offering an objective view into the human mind, such a perspective is a matter of faith. Neuroimaging is limited to merely observing people's physical nature.

It is only logical to place one's faith in neuroimaging to offer a picture of the mind if a person believes the materialistic idea that the mind and the brain are one in the same. Specifically, neuroscientists, neurologists, and other physicians can use Electronic imaging machines (such as electroencephalograms [EEGs] and magnetic resonance imaging [MRIs]) to produce images of the brain that make matters of faith concerning the mind seem to be matters of science. By providing a picture of the brain and comparing images, medical professionals have convinced many that they better understand the mind and have proven the theory of mental illness. To the observer of such photos, it appears as though faith is not relevant. But underlying faith is still there: it is required to believe the underlying theory of materialism and the idea that neuro-technology can observe the mind.

The underlying belief in neuroimaging rests in the ability of scientific tools to view differences in the brain. These differences are interpreted through the lens of the brain-dysfunction theory while ignoring or rejecting that such changes could be the effects instead of the cause. Dr. Peter Breggin comments,

> Clearly, proving an association between a particular state of mind and a particular reaction in the brain doesn't indicate which came first. Yet the biopsychiatrists, without discussing it, usually assume that the brain is the egg from which the chicken—mental disorder—is born. They search for signs of hyperactivity in the dopamine system of schizophrenics without acknowledging that if they find it, it could be the normal response of a normal brain to the prolonged expression of an intense emotional state.[113]

Furthermore, we must reiterate: viewing the physical brain is not a study of the spiritual mind. Yet, it is common practice in many medical books and journals to observe two images that compare a normal brain with an abnormal brain which is said to prove a theory of mental illness. For example, in 2004 in was suggested that neuroimaging could provide a new diagnostic tool to identify the psychiatric idea of bipolar disease:

> Researchers using a special type of imaging that tracks brain chemicals are able to produce a "chemical fingerprint of bipolar disorder," a development that may lead to earlier diagnosis and aid in treatment . . . . MR spectroscopy uses ordinary MRI technology that is modified to view the chemical properties of brain tissue and thus theoretically can detect the chemical changes associated with bipolar disorder as well as other mental illnesses.[114]

But providing images of chemical properties of brain tissue is not the same as viewing mental processes nor does it prove that the chemical changes are caused by an alleged mental illness.

---

[113] Breggin, *Toxic Psychiatry*, 112.

[114] Peggy Peck, Reviewed by Charlotte E. Grayson Mathis, "New Brain Scan May Diagnose Bipolar Disorder: Technique Tracks Chemical Changes in the Brain," *WebMd Health News*, (Nov. 30, 2004). http://www.webmd.com/bipolar-disorder/news/20041130/new-brain-scan-may-diagnose-bipolar-disorder

Neuroimages seemingly eliminate the need of faith, yet as we have seen, faith is the empowering reality behind neuro-determinism and the interpretations of these images. Years later, there still remains no biological marker to prove alleged bipolar.

The more modern brain-dysfunction theory which builds upon Kraepelin's original idea of determinism by the use of imaging technology is sometimes referred to as *neurocentrism*. Satel and Lilienfeld explain this new concept as

> the view that human experience and behavior can be best explained from the predominant or even exclusive perspective of the brain. From the popular vantage point, the study of the brain is somehow more "scientific" than the study of human motives, thoughts, feelings, and actions. By making the hidden visible, brain imaging has been a spectacular boon to neurocentrism."[115]

But the mind is and always will be hidden from brain scans.

Though the underlying theory of determinism is not new, the visible pictures that brain scans and MRIs provide of neurological activity of the brain enable a deeper faith in the old philosophical ideas of materialism. These photos seemingly give visible proof of what normal behavioral patterns and thoughts look like in the brain and how abnormal behaviors manifest in the brain's neurological makeup. Lieberman states,

> [The CAT scan] contained an astounding finding: the very first physical abnormality in the brain associated with one of the three flagship mental illnesses. Johnstone found that the brains of schizophrenic patients had enlarged lateral ventricles, a pair of chambers deep within the brain. Psychiatrists were thunderstruck. Ventricular enlargement was already known to occur in neurodegenerative diseases like Alzheimer's when the brain structures surrounding the ventricles began to atrophy, so psychiatrists *naturally inferred* the ventricular enlargement in schizophrenic brains was *due to atrophy from some unknown process* [emphasis added.][116]

---

[115] Satel and Lilienfeld, *Brainwashed*, introduction xix.

[116] Jeffrey A. Lieberman, *Shrinks: the Untold Story of Psychiatry* (New York: Little, Brown and Company, 2015), 209.

Lieberman recognizes that there are many unknowns in brain scans that must be interpreted and accepted by faith rather than observation; the "unknown process" of the brain shrinking in those labeled as schizophrenic is just as likely a result of childhood trauma or guilt,[117] deceptive thinking,[118] or fantasies.[119] But secularists want to dogmatically establish the atrophied brain as the cause of mental illness and not as one effect of spiritual mind.

Herein lies one of the major limitations of neuroimaging: it cannot reveal causes and effects — those must be inferred — or evaluate experiences and thoughts. Dr. John Abramson explains, "According to the philosopher John Searle, subjective experience and consciousness are not the kinds of things that can be studied directly by the roots of science — they can only be experienced."[120] If what is occurring in the mind is truly to be understood, it must be studied through Scripture and relationships rather than through neuroimaging or neuroscience. Clinical psychologist Richard Bentall explains,

> In short, the success of functional imaging studies usually depends on having a reasonable understanding of the psychological processes that are being imaged. In the absence of such an understanding, functional neuroimaging research is somewhat reminiscent of the nineteenth-century pseudoscience of phrenology, which tried to

---

[117] "Feelings of Guilt during Childhood Linked to Mental Illness," http://www.huffingtonpost.com/2015/01/07/guilt-mental-health_n_6423434.html?cps=gravity_2692_-376788313446572831.

[118] Whitfield, *Truth about Mental Illness*, 56.

[119] Elyn Saks, *The Center Cannot Hold: My Journey through Madness* (New York: Hachette Books, 2007), 51.

[120] Abramson, *Overdosed America*, 207.

locate mental functions in different regions of the brain by mapping bumps on the scalp. [121]

A scientific tool simply does not exist that can observe the mind. Lieberman, then, notes correctly that conclusions about brain scans are "inferred." [122] In other words, neuroimaging does not prove that mental illness is biological. It does not observe the spiritual mind, nor does it reveal causes of neural activity; it simply provides pictures of the current condition of the brain and the neurological activity in the brain at a moment in time. Psychiatrist Sally Satel and psychologist Scott Lilienfeld explain,

> The illuminated brain cannot be trusted to offer an unfiltered view of the mind. Nor is it logical to regard behavior as beyond an individual's control simply because the associated neural mechanisms can be shown to be "in the brain." [123]

Many general practitioners, psychiatrists, and functional neurologists are now charging large sums of money to conduct MRIs and EEGs on children; they assert that these types of medical scans can be used for diagnosing things such as ADHD, bipolar, and schizophrenia in children. But the *DSM* itself dismisses this practice:

> No biological marker is diagnostic for ADHD. As a group, compared with peers, children with ADHD display increased slow wave electroencephalograms, reduced total brain volume on magnetic resonance imaging, and possibly a delay in posterior to anterior cortical maturation, *but these findings are not diagnostic* [emphasis added]. [124]

---

[121] Bentall, *Madness Explained*, 163.

[122] Lieberman, *Shrinks*, 209.

[123] Satel and Lilienfeld, *Brainwashed*, 150.

[124] APA, *DSM-5*, 61.

The reality is that cause and effect are tricky subjects within brain science and even more so within the study of the mind where scientists lack tools to study the spiritual nature.

Although neuroimaging provides a visual tool for observing brain activity, blood flow, and brain size, CAT scans, MRIs, and EEGs, these tools are not diagnostic tools or biological markers neither do they in any way prove or disprove the secular construct of mental illness. In the same manner, these neuroimages do not prove or disprove God's wisdom concerning human behavior, mindsets, or emotions; they simply provide a snapshot of the brain and neural activity.

Furthermore, neuroimaging is limited in that it lacks the ability to explain motive, desire, intentions, maturation rates, beliefs, and a person's history to name a few. Dr. Bentall explains,

> Abnormal activations in patients may simply reflect the fact that they are not cooperating, are poorly motivated, or are doing something else. In fact . . . psychiatric patients often are poorly motivated when attempting psychological tests such as the Wisconsin Card Sort, and their performance can sometimes be dramatically improved by providing them with an incentive. Suspicion that this kind of problem can affect neuroimaging research is fuelled by the observation that hypofrontal patients sometimes show normal brain activations after a course of appropriate training on the relevant psychological tests.[125]

Causes and effects cannot be dogmatically determined from brain scans unless the object being studied (such as a bullet lodged in the brain) is shown in the brain scan. Even then, things like motive, fear, guilt, and mental processes must still be considered apart from neuroimaging. Neural activity, brain size, brain waves, and blood flow are not enough to determine cause and effect when it comes to the mind. Neuroscientist Valenstein explains,

---

[125] Bentall, *Madness Explained*, 166.

The brains of some "normal" — people with no history of any mental disorder — may show signs of some excessive or deficient neurotransmitter activity. It needs to be recognized that even if a chemical abnormality were eventually found to be highly correlated with the incidence of a particular mental illness, it would not be clear how such a finding should be interpreted. It might well be that the chemical "abnormality" was caused by the stress or some behavioral peculiarity commonly associated with a particular mental illness, rather than having been the cause of that illness. It is also well known that psychotherapeutic drugs can be the cause of chemical abnormalities. The "cause" and the "effect" of a mental illness are routinely confused.[126]

Similarly, Dr. Abramson remarks,

Medical researchers observe with increasing sophistication the physical correlates of subjective experience, relying upon galvanic skin response (the lie detector test), electroencephalogram (EEG or brain wave) recordings, and functional MRIs of the brain. These objective observations can help us understand what kind of physical changes take place during different experiences, but they get us not a bit closer to understanding what it feels like to be that person whose brain we are observing, nor to understanding the meaning of the experience for that person. This is why the extra scientific qualities that define personhood (and contribute so much to the personal decisions that are usually the most important determinants of our health) tend to get discounted or diminished in the world of biomedicine.[127]

Though, as Dr. Abramson notes, "personhood is diminished in the world of biomedicine," one's personhood is the topic at hand in all constructs of mental illness. Dr. Bentall also comments,

As in the case of structural abnormalities, abnormal brain activity may, in the end, turn out to be a consequence of adverse experience rather than a product of some kind of biological insult or malfunction.[128]

While secularists claim dogmatic findings that prove cause and effect, such claims are unfounded and serve as necessary presumptions to ensure secular ideas and biomedical approaches continue their acceptance.

---

[126] Valenstein, *Blaming the Brain*, 4.

[127] Abramson, *Overdosed America*, 207.

[128] Bentall, *Madness Explained*, 167.

In spite of the very real limitations, many secularists still claim that neuroimaging will somehow bring understanding to their unproven theories and unanswered questions. While such technology seemingly takes a person's beliefs and transforms them into observable data, these advances in neuroscience have not changed any patient outcomes or answered any questions regarding etiology and remedies. Psychiatrist Sally Satel and clinical psychologist Scott Lilienfeld comment about Thomas Insel's (director of the NIMH) observation:

> As Insel observed in a sobering 2009 article, there is no evidence that the past two decades of advances in neuroscience have born witness to decreases in mental disorders' prevalence or to any impact on patient life span. The failure of brain-imaging techniques to have yet made major inroads into the cause and treatment of mental illness offers a necessary reminder for modesty in our expectations.[129]

Brain imaging simply cannot tell us that which is beyond what is seen in the photo. To claim anything as science which cannot be seen in the images amounts to conjecture and speculation. Scans can observe valid impairment and neural activity in the brain, but there is no evidence that these scans explain why the brain is functioning the way it is. In other words, etiology is not explained in neuroimaging, and scans are not diagnostic tools for mental illness as brain-dysfunction theorists imply. Likewise, the mind and moral character can never be physically observed through neuroimaging tools. In spite of this reality, many neurologists, neuroscientists, and psychiatrists are making "extravagant claims about what brain scans can tell us about the mind."[130] These claims are not scientific or medically sound; they are rather speculation and propaganda. What neuroimages do supply — which all sides of the issue can agree upon — is a photo

---

[129] Satel and Lilienfeld, *Brainwashed,* 23.

[130] Ibid., 24.

of the brain's condition at a singular point in time. Brain scans, blood tests, genetic studies and all other biological tests and tools can never provide an explanation of moral behavior/character. They do not prove that mental illness is brain-dysfunction, and they do not eliminate the necessity of faith to believe that the physical nature causes mental illness. These neuroimaging tools do, however, provide Kraepelinians with a new object of faith and a renewed hope in science to bring about answers.

CHAPTER 3 – THE MORAL NATURE OF BEHAVIOR

Foundational to the current neo-Kraepelinian system of mental health is the idea that behavior is an amoral product of a person's biological nature. In fact, brain-dysfunctionists claim that behavior is strictly a scientific endeavor since it can be observed, measured, and repeated. However, those who hold to a psychosomatic anthropology understand that all people are moral creations of God and that their moral behaviors are not separate from their spiritual nature. There exists a non-material aspect of human behavior that can only be spiritually discerned. Ecclesiastes 12:13-14 explains,

> Now all has been heard; here is the conclusion of the matter: Fear God and keep his commandments, for this is the duty of all mankind. For God will bring every deed into judgment, including every hidden thing, whether it is good or evil.

All behavior matters to God, and each person is responsible to obey God's commandments and to know Him.

Obedience, however, demands that a presuppositional law or moral standard first be established. In fact, no matter the approach to the idea of mental illness, every person must determine what behavior is moral (born out of the spiritual nature), what behavior is amoral (caused by the non-volitional physical nature) and whether motive and intent make behavior moral. These lines of demarcation establish important distinctions between denying or accepting responsibility for one's actions. Morality not only makes mankind responsible for certain behavior, it also establishes a standard of good and bad character.

As with the pressing need to determine a standard of normalcy, one must also establish whether people are responsible for some of their actions, all of their actions, or none of their actions. If people are not responsible for at least some of their actions, then there is no need for the criminal justice system, academic grading scales, social law, religions, or any achievement awards in sports programs, work environments, or schools. If however, people must be held accountable for at least a few of their actions, then a moral system is established whether acknowledged or not.

Determining Morality

Establishing or denying any moral system of motive and behavior, though, demands an established authority. This authority should be the expert on human behavior, and granted the privilege of defining morals—delineating moral and amoral behavior—and establishing a system of morality. Furthermore, this sovereign must be fully capable of maintaining and consistently enforcing the proposed moral system.

It is widely accepted that morality is a standard of or "conformity to ideals of right human conduct." This widely held definition means that human conduct is a matter of character.[131] The judicial system, religion, sociology, and the construct of mental illness all place great emphasis on behavior in judging a person and fitting him or her into a system. This process leads to an important question when human conduct or behavior is determined to be unacceptable or undesirable: is it mental illness, immorality, social deviance, or simply obnoxiousness? Additionally, who has the authority to decide what behavior

---

[131] Character is a synonym of morality. http://www.merriam-webster.com/dictionary/morality.

amounts to right human conduct and how should we label and categorize these deviances? These questions once again bring us to the necessity of faith and authority.

As we discussed in volume 2, the construct of mental illness is an antithetical moral system to God's scriptural declarations, and both of these approaches are fighting to be the lens by which society judges human behavior.[132] In fact, Dr. Abramson notes how behavior is merely a reflection of one's moral character and belief system:

> Rarely do people change lifelong patterns of behavior simply in response to a recommendation from a health professional, though it does happen occasionally and is certainly worth a try. More typically, *people's behaviors are anchored in their personal histories, social relationships, and cultural and economic circumstances: in what might be called a personal paradigm. Significant and lasting change in behavior often requires changing the deep assumptions that sustain this paradigm of self* [emphasis added]. If one of the goals of medical care is to prevent disease, then don't doctors have a professional responsibility to address the unique health needs, habits, and risks of each individual?[133]

We all have a "personal paradigm" or worldview that not only determines our behaviors and lifestyles, but also how we discern, judge, or diagnose others' behavior to be good or bad. But is it a doctor's responsibility to attempt to change a patient's worldview — or paradigm as Abramson calls it — or to change a person's behavior?

The APA represents one group of people who are attempting to establish themselves as the authority on human conduct, to establish a standard of and approach to behavior, to establish a materialistic/evolutionary worldview, and to establish a system to change people's behavior. Yet, as discussed in the previous volume, many secular practitioners attempt to

---

[132] Berger, *Spiritual Nature*, 65-78.

[133] Abramson, *Overdosed America*, 205.

deny the moral nature of humanity through the philosophies of materialism and determinism while still recognizing the need to establish a standard of acceptable behavior, a corresponding criminal system, and to hold some people accountable for their actions (e.g., terrorists). Evolutionary psychiatrist Thomas Szasz explains,

> Human beings are choice-making animals. The freedom to make choices is both a blessing and a curse . . . . Traditionally, it was one of the functions of religions to relieve people of choices. Today, psychiatry — pharmacracy and the therapeutic state — performs the same job . . . . Life is an unending series of choices and, therefore, "problems of living." Ordinary choices — such as what to have for breakfast — we ignore as trivial. Extraordinary choices — such as whether to kill ourselves — we dismiss as the symptoms of mental illness. The profession of psychiatry rests on, and caters to, the ubiquitous human desire to avoid and evade, indeed deny the very possibility of, morally "unthinkable" choices. We use the rhetoric of psychiatry to transform such choices into medical-technical problems and "solve" them by appropriate "medical treatments." This discourse is why deception is intrinsic to the principles of psychiatry, and coercion-as-cure to its practices.[134]

The APA's *DSM* is not void of morals; instead it seeks to establish a new standard of character and a new approach to perceiving and resolving unacceptable behavior and "unthinkable" choices.

God's authority is an antithetical alternative to the moral system of the APA founded on genuine altruism and grace. Scripture lays out many specific behaviors that God says either please Him or displease Him accompanied by imperative commands to obey them. Discerning whether or not behavior is moral or amoral is simple if God's authority is established over human wisdom and authority. Scripture declares that behavior is moral if (1) God commands or forbids people to act in a

---

[134] Thomas Szasz, *Psychiatry: The Science of Lies* (New York: Syracuse University Press, 2008), 112-13.

specific manner.[135] Adultery for example is explicitly a moral behavior because Exodus 20:14 states, "You shall not commit adultery." Behaviors that God specifically declares to be immoral and imperatively commands us to withstand will never be caused by biological malfunctions, defects, or injuries. (2) If our intentions, motives, or desires which produce behavior are opposed to God or exalt mankind above God, then our behavior is found to be immoral no matter how good it appears outwardly. Hypocrisy is one example of seemingly right moral behavior being practiced outwardly but with wrong and deceptive motives inwardly. From a human perspective, the Pharisees' behavior appeared to be righteous and good, but their actions were done from a heart that rejected God and thus they were judged to be immoral by God. Matthew 23:27 says, "Woe to you, scribes and Pharisees, hypocrites! For you are like whitewashed tombs, which outwardly appear beautiful, but within are full of dead people's bones and all uncleanness." The fact that motives, intentions, and desires are important and not just the observable actions make merely evaluating behavior to determine morality (whether a person is responsible or not) impossible. We can discern what is the character of another person by behavior (Proverbs 20:11; Matthew 7:16-20; 12:33), but our observations of outward manifestations are not always

---

[135] A distinction must be made between God's moral law given to all mankind throughout all of history versus His social law that He gives to specific individuals or communities for a period of time. The Old Testament contains many Jewish laws that were social in nature intended to reveal to the people of antiquity God's moral law. For example, the eating of specific animals was forbidden within the Jewish culture, but in the New Testament God reveals that this law was not a moral law but a cultural or social law intended to both help those specific people and to reveal His holy character to them. Not all laws given in Scripture are universal moral laws.

accurate in discerning one's spiritual heart. On the other hand, if God declares behavior to be morally wrong, then the person's character is revealed to be morally reprehensible if they engage in such behavior no matter what excuse they might offer (e.g., pride, lying, stealing, and adultery always displease God even if intention is good or an excuse is offered).[136]

Christians recognize not only that humans are psychosomatic, but that God has established a clear law of morality for them to follow. In fact, Christians show God that they love Him by keeping his moral law (John 14:15). Granted, no one keeps His law perfectly, and these common failures often cause us and the societies in which we live great mental anguish, guilt, and distress. Our imperfection and inability to keep God's law does not make God's moral law irrelevant though. Instead, our falling short of God's standard makes His grace and His fulfillment of the law necessary — which is one of the key points the apostle Paul makes in the book of Romans. In spite of our moral failure, God has clearly established in His Word behaviors that both please and displease Him and behaviors that benefit others and build up society. Likewise, He has clearly established motives and desires that are acceptable to Him and others that He rejects. In fact, God's moral law that we love Him and love

---

[136] If children's valid physical impairments hinder them from hearing or understanding their parent's commands, then their behavior should never be considered disobedience. For example, children with severe down-syndrome (who do not function intellectually) should not be expected to understand complex commands let alone obey them. On the other hand, the theory of ADHD suggests that certain children are incapable of giving their attention unless they are interested. But there are no biological markers to validate such speculative claims concerning ADHD (see Daniel Berger II, *The Truth about ADHD: Genuine Hope and Biblical Answers* [Taylors, SC: Alethia International Publications, 2015]).

others undergirds all secondary commands (Matthew 22:36-37). Romans 13:9 says,

> For the commandments, "You shall not commit adultery, You shall not murder, You shall not steal, You shall not covet," and any other commandment, are summed up in this word: "You shall love your neighbor as yourself."

God does not accept a plea of insanity, the idea of psychosis, or the speculative claim of brain-dysfunction for breaking His moral law. If love is moral as God asserts, then relationships will be significant in both keeping God's law and our mental stability — a point that will be developed further in the next volume. To suggest a new moral system that differs even slightly from God's Holy Word, however, is to establish human wisdom as the moral authority and to establish a system that displeases God and marginalizes His grace and atoning sacrifice on the cross. Without necessary grace and God's merciful forgiveness, people must still find a remedy for their guilt, broken relationships, and moral failures. Morality is a foundational issue of any approach to the spiritual mind, alleged psychiatric disorders, and alleged abnormal behavior.[137]

Confounding Behavior

Within its construct of mental illness, the American Psychiatric Association (APA) has lumped valid physical impairments and damage to the brain together with their hypotheses about moral mindsets and behavior. Valid physiological problems such as communication disorders, learning disorders, some sleep disorders, autism, and dementia/amnesia, and other neurocognitive disorders are not moral issues, but do impair social interaction, mental function,

---

[137] Frances, *Saving Normal*, 17.

and quality of life. These physiological problems are known brain malfunction, damage, or sensory impairment and not caused by wrong thinking, misplaced desires, improper reactions, or lack of self-control to name a few. In other words, physiological problems are not mental struggles let alone illnesses.

By combining valid brain/neurological damage or deterioration together with hypothesized brain-dysfunctions and alleged genetic disorders in the *DSM*, secularists can use the clear validity of brain damage/deterioration to seemingly support their subjective theories as valid and trustworthy. Of course valid brain damage and physical impairments can affect the mind, but the effects of such impairment are very different from what secularists theorize to be brain-dysfunction or mental illness.

A closer examination of these valid physical impairments reveals that no immoral behavior is ever produced by the brain's deterioration or defects. Immoral behavior is always the result of one's spiritually depraved nature, which everyone — including those with valid physical impairments — has. For example, dementia and Alzheimer's disease are valid physical problems with biological markers and symptoms:

> While symptoms of dementia can vary greatly, at least two of the following core mental functions must be significantly impaired to be considered dementia: Memory, Communication and language, Ability to focus and pay attention, Reasoning and judgment, and Visual perception.[138]

Sometimes symptoms of dementia can be reversed when the cause is treatable such as in thyroid problems or vitamin

---

[138] "What is Dementia?" http://www.alz.org/what-is-dementia.asp.

deficiencies.[139] The secular claim made in the *DSM* that dementia, Alzheimer's, and autism (to name a few) are mental illnesses is really a misnomer; the mind's amoral impairment is an effect of the brain's deterioration or injury and not the cause of the impairment. Alzheimer's and dementia are really brain deterioration, and autism is sensory nerve impairment/damage,[140] but none of these diseases are mental illnesses.

Alzheimer's provides a great example. Alois Alzheimer, a student of Emil Kraepelin, realized that what was occurring in the patients now identified as having Alzheimer's disease was the result of plaques and tangles on the brain which were observable under a microscope. This clear biological marker reveals not a mental disorder, but a neurodegenerative disease. Ironically, it was Emil Kraepelin, the father of the current construct of mental illness, who first referred to this brain disease as Alzheimer's disease in a psychiatric textbook.[141] Kraepelin's selection of the nomenclature is most likely why Alzheimer's continues to be incorrectly classified in the *DSM* as a mental illness.

---

[139] Ibid.

[140] The label of autism is used to diagnose valid sensory impairment. However, it has become a broad term that is being abused in diagnoses of many children who have very limited (if any) sensory impairment. Instead of physical maladies causing impairment, these children have behavioral problems stemming from their depraved nature. Sensory impairment is a valid physical limitation that affects the amoral functions of many children, but the autism spectrum is not well defined in the *DSM* — which enables misdiagnoses — nor is it a mental illness.

[141] "The Discovery of Alzheimer's Disease," *Dialogues in Clinical Neuroscience* 5, no. 1 (March 2003): 101–8, http://www.ncbi.nlm.nih.gov/pmc/articles/PMC3181715/.

Not only can clear biological markers—such as the plaques and tangles in Alzheimer's patients' brains—be observed in valid brain injury or disease, but the outworking behaviors associated with valid brain injury, deterioration, or defects are amoral and specific. Breggin explains,

> Instead of metaphors laced with meaning, brain-damaged people typically display memory difficulties as the first sign that their mind isn't working as well as it once did. They have trouble recalling recently learned things, like names, faces, telephone numbers, or lists. Later they may get confused and disoriented as they display what is called an organic brain syndrome. In fact—and this is very important—advanced degrees of brain disease render the individual unable to think in such abstract or metaphorical terms. The thought processes that get labeled schizophrenia require higher mental function and therefore a relatively intact brain. No matter how bizarre the ideas may seem, they necessitate symbolic and often abstract thinking. That's why lobotomy 'works': the damage to the higher mental centers smashes the capacity to express existential pain and anguish.[142]

Genuine brain diseases should be distinguished from speculated brain-dysfunction in that higher mental function is directly attacked in valid brain diseases and injuries. Simply acting crazy, feeling crazy, or thinking crazy (however people subjectively assess that) does not mean that there is a biological disease present at all.

Autism, brain-damage, strokes, concussions, dementia, Alzheimer's, encephalitis, and so forth are never the cause of immoral thoughts or behavior. Instead, valid neurodegenerative diseases or impairments cause amoral physical symptoms such as speech impairment, memory loss, intellectual impairment, sensory impairment, and impaired motor skills.[143] These amoral effects of the brain's malfunction or deterioration do affect

---

[142] "Alois Alzheimer (1864-1915) and the Alzheimer Syndrome," *Journal of Medical Biography* 19, no. 1 (Feb. 2011): 32-33, http://www.ncbi.nlm.nih.gov/pubmed/21350079.

[143] Susan L. Mitchell, "Advanced Dementia," *New England Journal of Medicine* 372 (June 25, 2015): 2533-40.

people's mental capabilities, but they never cause mankind to think or act in a sinful way; for example, Alzheimer's disease does not cause people to steal, to lose their temper, or to cheat on their spouse. Those wrong mindsets and behaviors are always the result of a person's depraved nature.

But brain damage does sometimes reveal the spiritual heart's contents more easily. For example, a boxer who in his later life suffers from brain damage can be verbally or physically angry and violent, even harming those around him. But his anger and violent behavior is the direct result of his depraved heart. After all, like all humanity, he is a sinner. When we are healthy, we can better hold our temper and not lose it. But when we are physically impaired or challenged, our true nature is more easily revealed. Scripture commands believers to be angry, but not to sin (Ephesians 4:26), and Proverbs 29:22 says that "a man of wrath stirs up strife, and one given to anger causes much transgression." Temporary restrained anger over sin is often a right mindset and an expected emotional response, but carrying out behavior that is sin against others is never justified (Matthew 5:21-22). Furthermore, just as anger is our true human nature, so too is violence. In the example of the boxer, he willfully participated in a violent sport for many years prior to experiencing the side-effects of his brain damage. There exists no evidence that valid brain issues ever cause someone to act contrary to God's moral will.

In contrast to secular bio-determinism, Scripture establishes the depraved nature (the works of the flesh) of every person living apart from Christ as determining their moral choices and causing many of their problems. In true mental issues (e.g., what secularists refer to as anxiety, ADHD, delusions, bipolar, schizophrenia, and pedophilic disorders . . .) the Bible declares these to be spiritual in nature and products of the mind's deliberate choices. For example, within the proposed construct of bipolar disorder, pride, promiscuity, hopelessness, and lack of emotional/behavioral self-control are proposed effects of alleged brain-dysfunction. The *DSM* asserts about the construct of bipolar, "Sexual behavior may include infidelity or indiscriminate sexual encounters with strangers, often disregarding the risk of sexually transmitted diseases or interpersonal consequences."[144] But Scripture describes these behaviors as moral in nature, normal products of the depraved heart, and the responsibility of the believer in accordance with the work of the Holy Spirit (Galatians 5:22-25). In fact, Galatians 5:16-21 states,

> But I say, walk by the Spirit, and you will not gratify the desires of the flesh. For the desires of the flesh are against the Spirit, *and the desires of the Spirit are against the flesh, for these are opposed to each other, to keep you from doing the things you want to do* [emphasis added]. But if you are led by the Spirit, you are not under the law. Now the works of the flesh are evident: sexual immorality, impurity, sensuality, idolatry, sorcery, enmity, strife, jealousy, fits of anger, rivalries, dissensions, divisions, envy, drunkenness, orgies, and things like these. I warn you, as I warned you before, that those who do such things will not inherit the kingdom of God.

Secularists rename these desires and works of the flesh and claim that they are diseases to reflect their ideology (e.g., "alcoholism" and "oppositional defiant disorder" instead of "drunkenness" and "fits of anger/disobedience"),[145] but these desires and behaviors are normal human mindsets and activities apart from Christ and the work of the Holy Spirit.

The description of determinism that the Bible presents is an impairing moral condition of everyone apart from God's grace and not just a few. It is the spiritual flesh (the sinful nature)

---

[144] APA, *DSM-5*, 129.

[145] Bessel van der Kolk, *The Body Keeps the Score: Brain, Mind, and Body in the Healing of Trauma* (New York: Penguin Group, 2014), 27.

rather than the physical nature (brain and genes), which keeps people from behaving as they should and with a right motive to please God. This difference in anthropology is significant, as secularists see these behaviors as signs of abnormality, whereas God sees them as revealing the common human condition.

Although all people are born determined to sin against God and to pursue their own fleshly desires apart from His grace, everyone will be held accountable for both desire and the resulting behavior. Ecclesiastes 11:9 states not only that people will live or behave according to their spiritual desires, but also that God will judge each person for these pursuits: "Walk in the ways of your heart and the sight of your eyes. But know that for all these things God will bring you into judgment." It is not just our behavior that matters to God, but also our hidden motives or purposes for those actions. First Corinthians 4:5 explains,

> Therefore do not pronounce judgment before the time, before the Lord comes, who will bring to light the things now hidden in darkness and will disclose the purposes of the heart. Then each one will receive his commendation from God.

If our true motive or desire is to please God, then our moral behaviors will reflect this worthy pursuit (Ecclesiastes 9:10).

The sobering reality is that one's view of mental illness reveals his/her true moral values and perceived authority. How behaviors are perceived, where in one's being they are born, and where moral lines are drawn are all necessary elements to forming any theory about and approach to mental anguish and mental failures. Yet these important issues surrounding the human mind are first and foremost matters of faith.

CHAPTER 4 – THE BODY'S VALID IMPAIRMENTS

While psychiatry and neuroscience search for validation of their theories about the mind and mental struggles, genuine brain disease, visible brain damage, and physical impairments do help to shed light on the discussion. However, the truths that are revealed are not in favor of the secular construct of mental illness; rather, they expose the reality of the psychosomatic nature of humanity.

Valid Brain Injury

The brain is part of the central nervous system, and when the central nervous system is damaged, the peripheral nervous system is also negatively affected. This damage most often causes observable behavioral effects in the body. Valid brain or spinal cord injuries cause impairment and are detectable in three general ways: the sensory nerves, motor nerves, and autonomic nerves.[146] As we noted in the previous chapter, none of these impairments cause a person to fail morally.

It is also helpful to examine known brain injuries. There are currently six types of known brain injuries — all of which are recognizable through the peripheral nervous system's impairment: (1) Concussion — a blow or impact to the head that can cause swelling in the brain and even permanent damage. (2) Cerebral Contusion — a blow that bruises the brain, and Coup-Contracoup — a blow to the head that injures both sides of the brain. (3) Diffuse Axonal Injury– a violent movement or shaking

---

[146] "Peripheral Neuropathy: Potentially Disabling Nerve Problems," *Mayo Clinic Health Letter* 29, no. 10 (October 2011): 2.

that causes nerve tissues in the brain to tear. (4) Penetration — an object enters the skull and penetrates the brain. (5) Anoxia — a lack of oxygen to the brain. (6) Hypoxia — a lack of blood flow to the brain.[147]

In valid brain injuries the mental processes are altered sometimes temporarily and sometimes permanently. Yet these mental effects look very different from the proposed mental problems suggested in psychiatric disorders. True mental impairment due to valid brain injury, genetic defects, or brain illness produces amoral behavior and impairs normal mental processes:

> A mild traumatic brain injury is diagnosed only when there is a change in the mental status at the time of injury — the person is dazed, confused, or loses consciousness. The change in mental status indicates that the person's brain functioning has been altered.[148]

The National Institute of Neurological Disorders and Strokes describes symptoms of traumatic brain injuries this way:

> A person with a mild TBI may remain conscious or may experience a loss of consciousness for a few seconds or minutes. Other symptoms of mild TBI include headache, confusion, lightheadedness, dizziness, blurred vision or tired eyes, ringing in the ears, bad taste in the mouth, fatigue or lethargy, a change in sleep patterns, behavioral or mood changes, and trouble with memory, concentration, attention, or thinking. A person with a moderate or severe TBI may show these same symptoms, but may also have a headache that gets worse or does not go away, repeated vomiting or nausea, convulsions or seizures, an inability to awaken from sleep, dilation of one or both pupils of the eyes, slurred speech, weakness or numbness in the extremities, loss of coordination, and increased confusion, restlessness, or agitation.[149]

---

[147] N. Zasler, "Causes of Brain Injury," Brain Injury Association of America, *Brain Injury Source* 3, no. 3. See http://www.biausa.org/about-brain-injury.htm.

[148] Ibid.

[149] "Traumatic Brain Injury," http://www.ninds.nih.gov/disorders/tbi/tbi.html.

If a person's brain has been injured, the mind will be influenced and even impaired, but not in such a way that the person behaves immorally because of the injury. The brain-dysfunction theory underlying many so called mental illnesses simply does not add up to the empirical evidence available concerning valid brain injury or impairment.

As with valid brain injuries, birth defects, genetic defects, and neurodegenerative diseases do not cause moral failure. Physical disabilities, such as *Intellectual Disabilities* (once called mental retardation and which include *Down Syndrome*, *Fragile X*, and *Fetal Alcohol Syndrome* . . .), express mental impairment in two specific ways:

> [1] Intellectual functioning. Also known as IQ, this refers to a person's ability to learn, reason, make decisions, and solve problems.[2] Adaptive behaviors. These are skills necessary for day-to-day life, such as being able to communicate effectively, interact with others, and take care of oneself.[150]

Intellect, hygiene, learning, and communication are all affected by such physiological diseases, but these disabilities do not account for any moral failure. One must consider that the child is still depraved like all people; though mentally impaired with a disability, his or her depraved nature is still capable of producing immoral behavior. When children have a mild disability, they often are able to express their depraved nature as healthy children do. Angry outbursts and temper-tantrums, for example, are common occurrences in all children. There is even debate within the mental health field on whether or not anger outbursts are mental abnormalities or normal human behavior:

> A mental disorder whose symptoms include lashing out in aggressively verbal or violent ways [intermittent Explosive Disorder (IED)] has recently been found to be nearly twice as common as

---

[150] "Intellectual Disability," http://www.webmd.com/parenting/baby/intellectual-disability-mental-retardation.

previously thought. The research has sparked debate within the psychological community about the diagnosing of a mental illness whose symptoms overlap with normal, if undesirable, human behaviors, as well with as symptoms of other disorders.[151]

If one perceives undesirable behavior to be mental illness and humanity to only be material, then any unacceptable behavior must be attributed to some type of disease entity.

Valid Physiological Impairment

In addition to valid brain injury or defects, there also exist other physical influences that can impair a person's amoral thinking. We must again make it clear, however, that these physiological impairments affect the mind rather than cause the mind to think poorly or produce immoral behavior. The difference in *affect* and *cause* is not merely an issue of semantics, but one that changes who or what is responsible. A person's depraved nature is always responsible for his or her immoral character and behavior, so when one acts immorally, it should not be considered an abnormality but the normal product of a depraved heart. However, diets, habits, exercise, sleep deprivation, sickness, and physical pain to name a few can all directly influence or affect his or her thinking. Sleep deprivation and prescription medication represent two of the most profound and relevant examples.

Sleep Deprivation

While the mind is the governing agent in our moral executive functions, God designed the body to need rest in order to function properly. From the beginning of creation prior to the fall, this pattern was established in God's weekly structure and

---

[151] Remy Melina, "Is Rage a Mental Disorder?" http://www.livescience.com /9978-rage-mental-disorder.html (July 21, 2010).

the earth's orbit around the sun. God commanded mankind to rest on the seventh day, and He distinguished night from day. Sleep is not only God's will for mankind, but it is God's common goodness, as it is important to properly maintaining a person's physical and spiritual natures.

Sleep is so important that when people are deprived of sleep the mind and body are greatly affected. Psychologist F.C. Bartlett emphasizes the psychological impact of physical exhaustion in combat: "In war there is perhaps no general condition which is more likely to produce a large crop of nervous and mental disorders than a state of prolonged and great fatigue."[152] Likewise, psychiatrist Bessel van der Kolk writes,

> If your sleep is disturbed or your bowels don't work, or if you always feel hungry, or if being touched makes you want to scream (as is often the case with traumatized children and adults), the entire organism is thrown into disequilibrium. It is amazing how many psychological problems involve difficulties with sleep, appetite, touch, digestion, and arousal. Any effective treatment for trauma has to address these basic housekeeping functions of the body.[153]

The National Institute of Neurological Disorders also found that sleep deprivation greatly influences human behavior (which, in turn, can influence relationships):

> Sleep appears necessary for our nervous systems to work properly. Too little sleep leaves us drowsy and unable to concentrate the next day. It also leads to impaired memory and physical performance and reduced ability to carry out math calculations. If sleep deprivation continues, hallucinations and mood swings may develop. Some experts believe sleep gives neurons used while we are awake a chance to shut down and repair themselves. Without sleep, neurons may become so depleted in energy or so polluted with byproducts of normal cellular activities that they begin to malfunction. Sleep also

---

[152] F.C. Bartlett quoted by Dave Grossman, *On Killing*, 68.

[153] Van der Kolk, *Body Keeps the Score,* 56.

may give the brain a chance to exercise important neuronal connections that might otherwise deteriorate from lack of activity.[154]

Hallucinations involving all senses are said to be the product of sleep deprivation. Neurologist Oliver Sacks explains,

> When medical residents, for example, are on call for long periods, sleep deprivation may produce a variety of hallucinations involving any sensory modality. One young neurologist wrote to me that after being on call for more than thirty hours, he would hear the hospital's telemetry and ventilator alarms and sometimes after arriving home he kept hallucinating that the phone was ringing.[155]

Although lack of sleep will never cause anyone to morally fail, it can certainly impair one's judgment, perception, memory, performance, mental clarity, and emotional stability.[156] The mind and the nervous system are clearly influenced in an amoral way by one's quality and quantity of sleep. A recent article in the *Harvard Medical School Journal* helps to confirm this reality by revealing that naps "provide measurable cognitive benefits."[157]

Many times the observable behavior is heavily influenced by poor sleep or sleep deprivation, but it is diagnosed by clinicians as a mental illness. Take for example the psychiatric label of ADHD. Research shows that chronic poor sleep results in daytime tiredness, difficulties in focusing attention, behavioral self-control, emotional self-control, and increases impulsive

---

[154] National Institute of Neurological Disorders and Strokes, "Brain Basics: Understanding Sleep," http://www.ninds.nih.gov/disorders/brain_basics/understanding_sleep.htm.

[155] Oliver Sacks, *Hallucinations* (New York: Random House, 2012), 65.

[156] Gina Shaw, "Heavy Duty Stress among Kids of All Ages Is at an All-Time High. Why?" *WebMD magazine*, September 2015, 63.

[157] "Napping Boosts Sleep and Cognitive Function in Healthy Older Adults," *Harvard Women's Health Watch* 19, no. 1 (September 2011): 6.

activity.[158] Additionally, anxiety, antisocial behavior, and expressed anger are found to be increased in children when sleep deprivation is present.[159] This is not to say that sleep deprivation causes these behaviors, rather that lack of sleep influences one's ability to self-regulate. These behaviors — especially if they are chronic — often lead secularists to diagnose children as having the secular constructs of ADHD and ODD.

Sleep is an important part of God's design for people to experience wellness, and lack of sleep can promote mental and physical deterioration. So important, that the apostle Paul describes "sleepless nights" as part of a list of ways in which he had suffered: "As servants of God we commend ourselves in every way: by great endurance, in afflictions, hardships, calamities, beatings, imprisonments, riots, labors, sleepless nights, and hunger (2 Corinthians 6:4-10)." Sleep deprivation is in the same biblical category as suffering, affliction, and hardships.

While many factors can influence a person's sleep, research reveals that quality sleep greatly benefits people emotionally, physically, behaviorally, and spiritually. For example, many secular studies conclude that quality of sleep directly affects people's emotional states.[160] Psychiatrist Bessel van der Kolk remarks,

---

[158] R.E. Dahl, "The Impact of Inadequate Sleep on Children's Daytime Cognitive Function," *Seminars in Pediatric Neurology* 1 (Mar 3, 1996): 44-50.

[159] Kathryn Turnbull, Graham J. Reid, and J. Bruce Morton, "Behavioral Sleep Problems and their Potential Impact on Developing Executive Function in Children," *Sleep* 36, no. 7 (July 1, 2013): 1077-84.

[160] R. Cartwright, et al., "REM Sleep Reduction, Mood Regulation and Remission in Untreated Depression," *Psychiatry Research* 121, no. 2 (2003): 159-67.

Research had already shown that sleep, and dream sleep in particular, plays a major role in mood regulation. As the article in *Dreaming* pointed out, the eyes move rapidly back and forth in REM sleep, just as they do in EMDR [a form of hypnosis[161]]. Increasing our time in REM sleep reduces depression, while the less REM sleep we get, the more likely we are to become depressed.[162]

Similarly, Dr. Alan Watkins comments,

Each person needs to become aware of the quantity and quality of sleep he requires. Sleep reduces excess catecholamine and cortisol activity and helps the overworked, overdistended left ventricle to return to a proper size. Furthermore, adequate sleep enables emotion and effort to be handled in a much less demanding way.

---

[161] *Eye Movement Desensitization and Reprocessing Therapy* (EMDR) is a psychotherapy that combines a simulation of REM (Rapid Eye Movement) sleep with counseling that attempts to reshape one's thinking of traumatic events. The theory is that by suggesting new ways of thinking about traumatic experiences combined with rapid eye movements (or other physical stimulants), ongoing stress can be reduced and new memories formed about past traumatic experiences. The external sensory stimuli used in EMDR represents the difference between EMDR and cognitive therapy. The most common exercise utilized by clinicians in EMDR therapy is to have the individual move his or her eyes left and right as fast as possible — often referred to as "bilateral stimulation." While EMDR appears to be a new type of therapy, many feel that it is simply a new form of hypnotization. The therapy consists of eight phases: (1) information gathering, (2) desensitization through REM, (3-6) cognitive retraining: forming a different view of themselves, their circumstances, and their memories, (7) journaling, (8) and preparation and planning for future distressful situations (See hhtp://www.emdr.com/what-is-emdr/). For further study, see F. Shapiro, *Eye Movement Desensitization and Reprocessing: Basic Principles, Protocols, and Procedures* (New York: Guilford Press, 2001). In REM sleep, memories are often accessed and utilized in a person's dreams. The body also uses REM sleep to clean the brain in a unique way, which differs from the lymph system that cleans the rest of the body. It is widely understood that there exists a biological benefit to the body and cognitive functions from the eyes rapid lateral movement during the REM phase of sleep. But "therapy" — which is another way of saying counseling or teaching—helps to change a person's spiritual mind. EDMR represents one type of secular psychosomatic therapy and may very well be a new form of hypnosis.

[162] Van der Kolk, *Body Keeps the Score,* 260.

Consequently the general arousal level falls, reducing fatigue and easing the performance of daily activity.[163]

While neuroscientists know the basics of how many of these processes work and how important sleep is, they cannot fully explain all the complex details. What is clear, however, is that sleep directly affects one's motor skills, involuntary nervous system, mental clarity, and can even influence, not cause, poor decisions.

Getting rest is important to clear thinking and making right choices, but some people cannot sleep no matter what they do. Typically, though, lack of sleep is not the real problem but the side effect. So discovering the true cause of impaired sleep is important for mental stability and a healthy mind and body. We cannot assume that all sleep deprivation is caused singularly by either physical or spiritual issues.

Not being able to sleep can be caused by physical illness or pain, emotional hurt, spiritual guilt, real or imaginary fears, medications,[164] or sustained stress, to name a few.[165] Traumatic life events can also lead to lack of sleep. Soldiers coming back from the theater of war[166] who experienced traumatic or stressful events or mothers who sacrificially forgo sleep to care for their baby's needs should expect to have trouble sleeping and

---

[163] Alan Watkins, ed., *Mind-Body Medicine: A Clinician's Guide to Psychoneuroimmunology* (New York: Churchill Livingstone, 1997), 65.

[164] Sacks, *Hallucinations*, 192.

[165] Watkins, *Mind-Body Medicine*, 270-71.

[166] R. Greenberg, C. A. Pearlman, and D. Gampel, "War Neuroses and the Adaptive Function of REM Sleep," *British Journal of Medical Psychology* 45, no. 1 (1972): 27-33.

experience some form of impairment to their lives.[167] Dr. Sacks notes that many valid physical diseases can also cause sleep deprivation. Epilepsy[168] and Parkinson's[169] are two diseases where "chronic sleep deprivation" commonly occurs. These cases of lack of sleep are not caused by moral failure, but by valid physical reasons. Nonetheless, not getting sufficient and quality sleep will influence a person's thinking, judgment, and reactions.

Problems sleeping can also be the result of the spiritual heart. Ecclesiastes 2:23 says, "For all [man's] days are full of sorrow, and his work is a vexation. Even in the night his heart does not rest. This also is vanity." In some cases a person's inability to sleep is caused by his or her fear (anxiety), guilt, and or sin. For example, Proverbs 3:24 reveals that God's wisdom removes fear and makes sleep sweet: "When you lie down, you will not be afraid; When you lie down, your sleep will be sweet." Similarly, Psalm 4:8 states, "In peace I will both lie down and sleep; for you alone, O LORD, make me dwell in safety." While not all sleep deprivation or impairment is spiritual in nature, God's Word states that there is often a direct correlation between sleeping soundly and trusting God's wisdom/accepting His peace.

---

[167] Van der Kolk, *Body Keeps the Score*, 46.

[168] Sacks, *Hallucinations*, 138.

[169] Ibid., 83.

Still in other cases, prescription medications which allegedly treat mental illnesses are known to cause sleep deprivation.[170] For example, Ritalin and Dexedrine, which allegedly treat ADHD, are known to inhibit sleep in children. Research indicates that children taking these drugs are two to three times more likely to have problems sleeping, a significant percentage by anyone's standard.[171] Physicians explain this common occurrence in the *Journal of Pediatric Psychology*: "In both acute and long-term clinical trials, parents have listed sleep problems as one of the most common and persistent side-effects of stimulant medication."[172] The reason is simple: psychostimulants do what they are supposed to do; they stimulate and "enhance the levels of arousal in the central nervous system (CNS) and autonomic nervous system (ANS)."[173] Normally people are stimulated through their senses or sensory nerves,[174] but drugs

---

[170] Judith Owens, "A Clinical Overview of Sleep and Attention-Deficit/Hyperactivity Disorder in Children and Adolescents," *Journal of the Canadian Academy of Child and Adolescent Psychiatry* 18, no. 2, (2009): 92–102.

[171] Reut Gruber, et al., "Performance on the Continuous Performance Test in Children with ADHD Is Associated with Sleep Efficiency," *Sleep* 30, no. 8 (Aug 1, 2007): 1003–9.

[172] Penny Corkum, et al., "Acute Impact of Immediate Release Methylphenidate Administered Three Times a Day on Sleep in Children with Attention-Deficit/Hyperactivity Disorder," *Journal of Pediatric Psychology* 33, no. 4 (October 9, 2008): 368–79.

[173] Gruber, et al., "Performance on the Continuous Performance Test in Children with ADHD Is Associated with Sleep Efficiency," *Sleep* 30, no. 8 (Aug 1, 2007): 1003–9.

[174] "Peripheral Neuropathy: Potentially Disabling Nerve Problems," *Mayo Clinic Health Letter* 29, no. 10, (October 2011): 1-3.

provide a stimulation that does not shut down as the senses do when a person is sleeping. Thus the child remains in a heightened and aroused state as long as the drugs are in his or her system. This reality poses a logical and ethical problem for physicians to use a drug that knowingly hinders sleep which in turn hinders attention:

> The relationship between sleep problems and ADHD is hardly a straightforward one, and may present clinically in a number of different guises. For example, psychotropic medications used to treat ADHD or comorbid psychiatric conditions associated with ADHD (i.e., mood disorders, anxiety) may themselves result in sleep problems in some patients, daytime manifestations of primary sleep disorders such as obstructive sleep apnea may "mimic" ADHD symptomatology in others, comorbid sleep problems may exacerbate ADHD symptoms, and/or sleep problems may in some cases represent an "intrinsic" dysregulation of sleep and wakefulness associated with ADHD-related CNS dysfunction.[175]

In fact overwhelming evidence indicates that lack of sleep can influence one's ability to pay attention.

> Thus, from a clinical standpoint, sleep difficulties in children with ADHD not only potentially have a direct negative impact on the nature and severity of daytime ADHD symptoms as well as the quality of life for these patients, but they present a considerable challenge for the clinician in elucidating the nature and etiology of the sleep problems and in developing effective treatment strategies . . . From a theoretical perspective, there is substantial empirical evidence supporting an overlap in those central nervous system centers that regulate sleep and those that regulate attention/arousal, suggesting disruptions in one system might well have parallel effects on the other. Furthermore, similar perturbations in neurotransmitter pathways, particularly noradrenergic and dopaminergic systems, are found in both ADHD and sleep disturbances.[176]

In some cases, children who are labeled as having ADHD and who have trouble paying attention in school may actually be deprived of quality sleep. When stimulants are prescribed to allegedly treat the problem of inattention, the drugs may

---

[175] Owens, "Overview of Sleep and Attention-Deficit/Hyperactivity Disorder," 92–102.

[176] Ibid.

actually exacerbate the true problem and further impair the child's ability to sleep.

Sleep is one of the most fundamental and necessary activities that all people need, yet most people do not get enough. While sleep can certainly influence our thinking, affect our emotions, and impact our behavior, lack of sleep will never cause us to think or act immorally, and it never provides an excuse to behave in a way that displeases God and harms others.

Prescription Medications

The negative effects of impaired sleep are not the only valid physical problem that psychotropic drugs create. There is substantial evidence that many psychotropic drugs damage the brain and nervous systems. Dr. Robert Whitaker explains the assertion made by neuroscientist and former director of the NIMH, Steve Hyman, that

> Antipsychotics, antidepressants, and other psychotropic drugs . . . "create perturbations in neurotransmitter functions." In response, the brain goes through a series of compensatory adaptations. If a drug blocks a neurotransmitter (as an antipsychotic does), the presynaptic neurons spring into hyper gear and release more of it, and the postsynaptic neurons increase the density of their receptors for that chemical messenger. Conversely, if a drug increases the synaptic levels of a neurotransmitter (as an antidepressant does), it provokes the opposite response: The presynaptic neurons decrease their firing rates and the postsynaptic neurons decrease the density of their receptors for the neurotransmitter. In each instance, the brain is trying to nullify the drug's effects. "These adaptations are rooted in homeostatic mechanisms that exist, presumably, to permit cells to maintain their equilibrium in the face of alterations in the environment or changes in the internal milieu."[177]

Long term effects of psychotropic drugs alter not only the physical brain, but they can also cause "substantial and long-lasting alterations in neural function . . . qualitatively as well as

---

[177] Steve Hyman quoted by Robert Whitaker, *Anatomy of An Epidemic: Magic Bullets, Psychiatric Drugs, and the Astonishing Rise of Mental Illness in America* (New York: Broadway Books, 2015), 83.

quantitatively different from the normal state."[178] In other words, psychotropic drugs that allegedly treat brain-dysfunction can actually create valid physical problems and abnormal brains from healthy ones. Such a reality led the psychiatrist Peter Breggin to state,

> It's quite ironic actually, because the only imbalances that we know of in the brains of people called mental patients are the ones inflicted on them by the psychiatric drugs. How ironic: we make a false claim that they have chemical imbalances and then we give them chemical imbalances.[179]

In a similar manner, Dr. Whitaker asserts,

> [Scientists] had a remarkably detailed understanding of neurotransmitter systems in the brain and of how drugs acted on them. And what science had revealed was this: Prior to treatment, patients diagnosed with schizophrenia, depression, and other psychiatric disorders do not suffer from any known "chemical imbalance." However, once a person is put on a psychiatric medication, which, in one manner or another, throws a wrench into the usual mechanics of a neuronal pathway, his or her brain begins to function, as Hyman observed, *abnormally* [his emphasis].[180]

In truth, abnormal brains are often created by alleged psychotropic remedies, and this common occurrence directly affects the mind and the rest of the body.[181] Sleep deprivation represents one example, but the *DSM* lists many of their mental and behavioral disorders as potentially being caused by the psychotropic medication that physicians prescribe: "Medication-

---

[178] Steve Hyman, "Initiation and Adaptation: A Paradigm for Understanding Psychotropic Drug Action," *American Journal of Psychiatry* 153 (1996): 151-61.

[179] The documentary: *Generation RX*, 7:10.

[180] Robert Whitaker, *Anatomy of An Epidemic: Magic Bullets, Psychiatric Drugs, and the Astonishing Rise of Mental Illness in America* (New York: Broadway Books, 2015), 84.

[181] APA, *DSM-5*, 96.

Induced Psychotic Disorder,"[182] "Medication-Induced Bipolar Disorder,"[183] and "Medication-Induced Depressive Disorder"[184] are three examples. Prescription medications which allegedly treat mental illness are known to damage the very organ they claim to treat and to create the very illness they allegedly heal. The bottom line is that valid brain injuries and defects and other valid and measurable physical impairments can influence one's thinking, but they will never cause immoral mindsets or behaviors.[185] Those failures are sourced in the moral/spiritual nature of each person.

---

[182] Ibid., 110.

[183] Ibid., 142.

[184] Ibid., 175.

[185] There continue to be claims that some murders and acts of violence occur because the murderer is mentally ill and could not help himself. Sometimes even valid brain damage is cited as causative. For example, in early 2016, McCann Utu killed both his mother and brother. The news presented the story that he must have suffered from mental illness since he had sustained two head injuries and had not been a violent person prior to that episode. The autopsy report, however, revealed that he had been taking antidepressants (http://www.nbcdfw.com/news/local/Plano-Teen-Who-Killed-Mother-Brother-Had-Taken-Anti-Depressant-ME-378431291.html), which are known to incite violence, murder, and sometimes even suicide (See Peter Breggin, *Medication Madness: The Role of Psychiatric Drugs in Cases of Violence, Suicide and Murder* [New York: St. Martin's Press, 2008]).

CHAPTER 5 – THE MIND'S EXECUTIVE CONTROL

The psychosomatic approach represents a viable alternative to the materialistic/strictly biological-anthropology and approach of secularists. Whereas Kraepelin's brain-dysfunction and genetic theories propose that an individual's biology determines his or her character and governs his or her life, recent research reveals that a person's mind and not his or her brain is the true executive governor over one's moral life.

Most everyone who accepts the psychosomatic nature of mankind agrees that the physical and spiritual natures are interrelated. However, some are unwilling to consider that the biological changes, impairments, and dysfunctions that occur in what are considered to be mental illnesses are observable and measureable effects of the mind's influence on the physical body and not an etiological explanation. Scientific research — supported by empirical evidence — is consistently revealing that people's thoughts change not only their life for better or for worse but also their physical nature. Though faith is required to hold to any anthropology, the psychosomatic approach is fully supported by empirical evidence observed in the mind's effects on the body.

Based on Faith

We must again make it clear that the psychosomatic position does not attempt to base its validity on scientific proof. Rather, each person must choose by faith to accept any theory of origins, approaches to anthropology, and subsequent views of mental illness (Hebrews 11:2b). In Jeremiah 17:9-10,[186] we find another important truth relevant to understanding and approaching mankind. That is, the passage establishes that we must either trust in human or divine wisdom to deal with our incredible deception and incurable spiritual heart.

In Jeremiah 17:5, God sets forth the only two options that people have to approach these issues: "Thus says the LORD: 'Cursed is the man who trusts in man and makes flesh his strength, whose heart turns away from the LORD.'" Jeremiah contrasts this choice in verse 7 with another promise: "Blessed is the man who trusts in the LORD, whose trust is the LORD." We only have two options in regards to our deceptive nature and incurable metaphorical sickness: we can trust in our own hearts and remain "cursed," or we can trust the one who alone can search the heart and mind and provide deliverance and mental restoration. Each of these choices has direct consequences: trusting in human wisdom brings further turmoil and deception (verse 6), and trusting in God brings freedom from anxiety, freedom from deception, and deliverance from the ultimate mental turmoil of condemnation. In 1 Chronicles 28:9-10 David charges his son with such truth:

> And you, Solomon my son, know the God of your father and serve him with a whole heart and with a willing mind, for the LORD searches all hearts and understands every plan and thought. If you seek him, he will be found by you, but if you forsake him, he will cast you off forever.

---

[186] The passage of Scripture where we discover the declaration of what God considers mental illness to be (metaphorically) and where we also learn that God alone can search a person's immaterial nature and judge his or her behavior (see also Revelation 2:23). The Jeremiah 17:9-10 states, "The heart is deceitful above all things, and desperately [incurably] sick; who can understand it? I the LORD search the heart and test the mind, to give every man according to his ways, according to the fruit of his deeds."

Though science cannot explore the mind itself, it can observe and repeat the mind's affects on the brain and body. This reality is why many neuroscientists are now attempting to understand the mind or mental functions in order to better understand the brain. Dr. Steven Novella remarks,

> The second major effort to redefine mental illness uses the latest (and continually developing) technology to image brain function. If we can identify the modules and networks in the brain that underlie specific mental functions, and then further identify networks that are behaving differently in patients with certain mental disorders, this may provide yet another way to reclassify and understand mental illness. In this effort, neuroscientists are stepping back from the *DSM*. The *DSM* is useful clinically, because it describes the problems with which people present. But perhaps it does not reflect the actual underlying brain malfunction. *So neuroscientists studying mental illness are trying to think about disorders in terms of basic mental functions, then identify the network in the brain that correlates with that function, and perhaps identify how it is misbehaving in people with a specific deficit* [emphasis added].[187]

Logically, if mental problems (what they call illnesses) are truly mental, then starting with the mind to understand the mind makes more sense than secularist's proposal to start with the brain in order to understand the mind. Of course, for those who only hold to science, studying the mind poses a real problem. More and more cognitive neuroscientists like Caroline Leaf understand that the mind must be the starting point in mental issues and discussions about the mind.[188] What determines one's starting point, however, is always their presuppositional worldview and subsequent anthropology. A person can either choose to start with speculative and ever-changing theories that are purported as scientific fact or start with the Creator's written immutable Word that precisely explains the human mind.

---

[187] Novella, "Genetics of Mental Illness."

[188] Leaf, *Switch on Your Brain.*

Evolutionists and those who hold to a biblical worldview both agree that the brain is actively involved in behavior, but they disagree over which nature (spiritual or physical) has executive control over our moral functions. The brain-dysfunctionist sees the brain as the ultimate source of behavior, whereas the creationist sees the spiritual heart (the central existence of self: soul, spirit, and mind) producing our moral behaviors.

Many neuroscientists and psychiatrists argue that since they can stimulate the brain through electric shocks (transcranial magnetic stimulation or TMS) to create the sensation of anxiety in the body, then anxiety must be sourced in the physical brain. However, these doctors and scientists fail to understand that what they produce through TMS is not actually anxiety, but the physical effects of anxiety. Anxiety — and all other mental processes — directly affect people's physical natures and often produce measurable and observable effects in the body.[189] Neuroscientists can identify the physical source of these affects and are correct in concluding that the brain is involved in all human behavior, but many are only willing — rather they are only capable within their deterministic mindset — to go back to the point of which they can observe the brain and neurons. But Scripture makes it clear that anxiety is a spiritual process that will manifest itself in the physical and observable nature (Philippians 4:6-7). Proverbs 12:25 states, "Anxiety in the heart of man causes depression, but a good word makes it glad (*NKJV*)." Whatever the physical effects might be, anxiety is sourced in the spiritual heart/mind.

---

[189] Caroline Leaf, *Who Switched off My Brain: Controlling Toxic Thoughts and Emotions* (South Lake, TX: Inprov, 2009).

Another way to understand this point is by observing human sexuality. Scripture presents sexuality as a moral issue that is carried out in the physical body (e.g., 1 Corinthians 6:15-19). When people choose to lust, their spiritual thoughts produce chemical, hormonal, and other physical changes to the body. TMS experiments can reproduce these physical effects if enough knowledge is available, but the effects are not equal to the thought processes. If an individual is diagnosed as having "pedophilic disorder" and lusts after children,[190] brain-dysfunction can be claimed as the cause and the individual's brain neurology mapped out to show abnormalities. Yet moral thoughts are behind this wrong and sinful thinking and explain the physical changes to the brain.

Here is a classic example of confusing causes with effects (or simply denying the true cause): the brain is a corollary to anxiety, but it is not the cause. In the example of TMS, electronically stimulating the parts of the brain that are affected by the mindset of anxiety does not prove the brain-dysfunction theory to be valid; it simply illustrates that the brain is involved in the physical effects of what anxiety does to the body. In essence, TMS experiments can recreate the physical symptoms of anxiety by stimulating the area of the brain which the mind naturally activates when a person is anxious. Nonetheless, one's worldview will determine whether he or she believes that the mind or the brain is the executive over his or her moral actions.

Based on Scientific Observation

The dualistic nature of mankind is fully supported by direct observation, repeatable studies, and a variety of scientific research. By using the scientific method, one can realize that the

---

[190] APA, *DSM-5*, 697.

mind is the chief executive of our moral behavior. Repeatable observations are foundational to the scientific process, but we have made it clear that the mind itself cannot be directly observed except by God (e.g., Jeremiah 17:9-10; Revelation 2:23). People can only spiritually discern the heart as they understand God's mind and declarations and observe the mind's effects on the body.

Therefore scientific observations must be understood to be effects of the mind on the brain, nervous system, and neuro-chemicals of the body and not an actual study of the mind. Yet, these scientific observations yield a consistent truth that the immaterial mind governs the physical body in moral matters. We will also observe that God's natural revelation (what science seeks to observe and form conclusions about) is in perfect harmony with God's supernatural revelation (His Word as illuminated by the Holy Spirit) in revealing the mind's control over our moral existence.

Although Scripture does not need validation, scientific observations provide further evidence of God's wise design of both people and the natural world. We are truly fearfully and wonderfully made (Psalm 139:14). What evidence reveals is that the brain is like any other part of the body and not the central moral and volitional intelligence that many secularists claim that it is. Former chief of brain biochemistry at the National Institutes of Health, Candace Pert, explains,

> Originally, we scientists thought that the flow of neuropeptides and receptors was being directed from centers in the brain — the frontal cortex, the hypothalamus, the amygdale. This fit our reductionist model, supporting the view that thoughts and feelings are products of neuronal activity, and that the *brain was the prime mover, the seat of consciousness* [the mind]. Then, as a result of my own and other people's work in the laboratory, we found that the flow of chemicals arose from many sites in the different systems simultaneously — the immune, the nervous, the endocrine, and the gastrointestinal — and that these sites formed nodal points on a vast superhighway of internal information exchange taking place on a molecular level. We then had to consider a system with intelligence diffused throughout, *rather than a one-way operation adhering strictly to the laws of cause and*

effect, as was previously thought when we believed that the brain ruled over all [emphasis added].[191]

Dr. Pert's comments not only dispel the brain-dysfunction theory, they also reveal the materialistic gospel to be a false system of belief. Instead of science revealing the brain to be the executive — or as she puts it "the prime mover," the bodily systems affect one another and are governed by a central "intelligence," which is the spiritual heart or mind. Scientific research is painting a different picture than materialists/ determinists are claiming. Professor of neurology and neurological surgery at Columbia University Dr. Stephan Mayer also states, "We're now sort of entering an era when we realize the brain is not that different from the rest of the body."[192] Likewise, physician and author, Alan Watkins remarks,

> The last 20 years have seen a rapid advance in scientific understanding of the immune system. The fact that many immune processes were originally demonstrated in a test tube, in vitro, led to the early assumption that the immune system was autonomous. However, PNI research has successfully challenged this assumption and a wealth of hard scientific data has provided irrefutable evidence that virtually all of the body's defense systems are under the control of the central nervous system (CNS). *Thus, every idea, thought and belief has a neurochemical consequence* [emphasis added].[193]

Others, like clinical psychologist Richard Bentall, agree:

> Psychological changes are always accompanied by changes in the Brain. Each new skill, or piece of information that we learn, is accompanied by the creation of new neural circuits that make new patterns of behaviour possible. These changes reflect the endless interaction between ourselves and the physical and social

---

[191] Pert, *Molecules of Emotion*, 310.

[192] Stephan Mayer quoted by Elizabeth Landau, "The Brain's Amazing Potential for Recovery," May 5, 2011, http://www.cnn.com/2011/HEALTH/05/05/brain. plasticity.giffords/index. html.

[193] Watkins, *Mind-Body Medicine*, 3.

95

environment in which we live. Put crudely, our brains are constantly being rewired in response to our experiences.[194]

It is becoming a growing trend and even commonplace in the scientific and medical communities to accept the fact that human faith and immaterial thoughts — both sourced in the immaterial mind — cause neurochemical and immune responses in the brain and the rest of the body. The clear evidence wrought from extensive research disproves the brain-dysfunction theory, materialism, and determinism as viable or necessary theories. In fact, the brain-dysfunction theory is not objective science nor does it enable good medical practices.

---

[194] Bentall, *Madness Explained*, 160.

CHAPTER 6 – THE BRAIN'S ABILITY TO CHANGE

For determinists, one of the most problematic scientific discoveries about the brain is that it is not fixed or unchangeable; it is characterized by plasticity. That is, the brain remodels, remaps, and can even reassign brain function to other non-impaired or healthy parts of the brain. Extensive research reveals that people with valid brain impairment have consistently shown the ability to remap sensory function to healthy parts of the brain. In some cases, near-full recovery has even occurred.

Neuroplasticity

Until the last thirty years, physicians and neuroscientists thought that specific areas of the brain accounted only for precise behavior and functions. For example, scientists identified the pre-frontal cortex or frontal lobes as the area of the brain where attention and perception occur. Dr. Candace Pert notes,

> Also known as the forebrain, [the frontal cortex] is unique to humans and sits behind the forehead. It is the location for all the higher cognitive functions, such as planning for the future, making decisions, and formulating intentions to change. . . . In short, the frontal cortex is what makes us truly human.[195]

Likewise, it is widely understood within neuroscience that the left and right hemispheres of the brain primarily control the opposite sides of the body. But when damaged or removed, the

---

[195] Candace B. Pert, *Molecules of Emotion: The Science behind Mind-Body Medicine* (New York: Scribner, 1997), 288.

brain can reassign these functions to other more healthy areas.[196]
This remapping is the benefit of the brain's neuroplasticity. Dr.
Eagleman's example of the girl who had half of her brain
removed but still functioned in near-full capacity provides one
example of this type of neuroplasticity.[197] Elizabeth Landau
comments,

> Alternatively, so-called "mirror neurons," located on the opposite
> side of the brain from the damaged area, can become involved in
> roles that the injured region used to have, he said. For instance, an
> injury to the left hemisphere of the brain, which in 95% of people
> controls the capacity to understand and generate language, doesn't
> necessarily mean the patient can never have a conversation again.
> That's because the right side of the brain can take over some
> language functions.[198]

Drs. Schwartz and Gladding further explain,

> Neuroplasticity includes any process that results in a change in the
> brain's structure, circuits, chemical composition, or functions in
> response to changes in the brain's environment. It is a property of
> the brain and is best understood as a capacity (or potential) for brain
> areas and circuits to take on new roles and functions.[199]

Another example of neuroplasticity can be observed in the case
of Gabrielle Giffords, member of the U.S. House of
Representatives from 2007-2012. Elizabeth Landau reports,

> Arizona Rep. Gabrielle Giffords is making a remarkable recovery
> after a gunshot wound to the brain, doctors say. Her case shows off

---

[196] Elizabeth Landau, "The Brain's Amazing Potential for Recovery," May 5,
2011, http://www.cnn.com/2011/HEALTH/05/05/
brain.plasticity.giffords/index. html.

[197] This example was offered in volume 2 in this series. David Eagleman, *The
Brain: The Story of You* (New York: Pantheon Books, 2015), 162.

[198] Landau, "Potential for Recovery."

[199] Jeffery Schwartz and Rebecca Gladding, *You Are Not Your Brain: The 4-
Step Solution for Changing Bad Habits, Ending Unhealthy Thinking, and Taking
Control of Your Life* (New York: The Penguin Group, 2011), 36.

the brain's capability to restore some functions after substantial injury, a phenomenon called "plasticity" that is helped by rehabilitation. "It's still a relatively new concept," said Dr. Sanjay Gupta, neurosurgeon and CNN chief medical correspondent. "The brain was once thought to be completely immutable" or not capable of change, after childhood. . . ."I'm still amazed from time to time at how well people do, and I think that we have simply underestimated the resilience and regenerative capacity in the human brain," said Dr. Stephan Mayer, professor of neurology and neurological surgery at Columbia University.[200]

But this brain phenomenon does not happen by chance and is not limited to people with damage or impairment. Rather, neuroplasticity occurs through repetition and habituation in all people. In other words, it is the process of education (or re-education). Begley comments on *neuroplasticity*: "By the middle of the twentieth century, then, neuroscientists had accumulated a compelling body of evidence that the brain is dynamic, remodeling itself continually in response to experience."[201] Experiences — especially repeated experiences — allow restructuring, healing, and education to occur. This phenomenon explains why habits can be realized, mastery can be achieved, and even addictions can be formed. Dr. Eagleman explains,

The brain is fundamentally unlike the hardware in our digital computers. Instead, it's "liveware." It reconfigures its own circuitry. Although the adult brain isn't quite as flexible as a child's, it still retains an astonishing ability to adapt to change[202]. Every time we learn something new . . . the brain changes itself.

The brain responds to one's thinking — including thoughts about life's experiences — and allows neuroplasticity to occur. This reality is one of the strongest reasons why physical therapy is so

---

[200] Landau, "Potential for Recovery."

[201] Sharon Begley, *Train Your Mind, Change Your Brain* (New York: Ballantine Books, 2007), 30.

[202] David Eagleman, *The Brain: The Story of You* (New York: Pantheon Books, 2015), 163.

often beneficial to those with physical impairments such as autism or speech impairments. But the brain's ability to change, adapt, remodel and heal itself opposes the bio-deterministic theories of mental illness that claim impairment is permanent or that it is one's destiny. If in fact dysfunction were found in the brain, then through neuroplasticity healing could also occur. We know this to be true, because neuroplasticity often occurs with valid brain damage — even when half the brain is surgically removed:

> The operation known as hemispherectomy — where half the brain is removed — sounds too radical to ever consider, much less perform. In the last century, however, surgeons have performed it hundreds of times for disorders uncontrollable in any other way. Unbelievably, the surgery has no apparent effect on personality or memory.[203]

While motor skills like speech, walking, and use of the opposite side of the body are impaired, a person's character is not affected. The reality that one's personhood is not found in their brain offers people who have been told that their brain is dysfunctional and unchangeable the hope that they can positively change. Dr. Leaf explains, "The fact that the brain is plastic and can actually be changed by the mind gives tangible hope to everyone, no matter what the circumstance."[204] Dr. Leaf goes on to point out that people with valid physical brain trauma, defects, and sensory impairments (such as autism) can all improve thanks to the plasticity of the brain.

---

[203] Charles Choi, "Strange but True: When Half a Brain is Better than a Whole One," Scientific American, May 24, 2007, http://www.scientificamerican.com/article/strange-but-true-when-half-brain-better-than-whole/.

[204] Leaf, *Switch on Your Brain*, 22.

Neuroplasticity, as Eagleman and Leaf note, is not limite

helping children recover.[205] Begley explains, "So convinced we.

neuroscientists that the adult brain is essentially fixed that they

largely ignored the handful of (admittedly obscure) studies

suggesting that the brain is actually malleable and shaped by

experience."[206] Experience, especially repetitive experiences play

a major role in neuroplasticity and shaping the brain and its

functions in all people.

Neuroplasticity is not very different from education. In fact,

when the brain or body is damaged or ill, physicians typically

refer to this habituation through repetition as "therapy" and

"treatment," and when the brain and body are perceived to have

normal function, professionals call this process of repetition and

habituation "education,""discipline," or "training." In other

words, neuroplasticity is a medical term used to describe a

damaged or impaired brain's ability to still learn, readapt, heal,

and get stronger.

From a physiological standpoint, people can be educated

because of the neuroplasticity of their brain. As with education,

neuroplasticity is made efficient through repetition and

experience. In an interview with neurosurgeon Stephan Mayer,

Elizabeth Landau reports,

> The goal of rehabilitation is to stimulate the brain to re-form lost
> circuits. In order to take advantage of the brain's plasticity, the
> patient must be placed in an environment where he or she is
> challenged constantly, Mayer said. "You need to be really actively
> engaged. You need to be working hard on trying to get back."[207]

---

[205] Ibid., 23.

[206] Begley, *Train Your Mind,* 31.

[207] Landau, "Potential for Recovery."

Similarly, Dr. Eagleman remarks on the importance of repetition in neural activity:

> To help children improve their self-control, the program provides a system of mentoring, counseling, and rewards. An important technique is to train them to pause and consider the future outcomes of any choice they might make — encouraging them to run simulations of what might happen — thereby strengthening neural connections that can override the immediate gratification of impulses. Poor impulse control is a hallmark characteristic of the majority of criminals in the prison system.[208]

Likewise, neuroscientist James Zull explains the process of education from a neurological vantage point:

> What the title ["The Art of the Changing Brain"] *says is that learning is a physical change in the brain* [emphasis added]. This is one thing neuroscience has shown us, and if it is true, then it must be that successful teachers produce change in the learner's brain. But generating that change is not a science; it is an art. In other words, science may tell us what learning is, and what influences it, but to apply this knowledge effectively is nothing if not an art![209]

If determinism were true and teachers bore the responsibility of altering the brains of their students, then the grading scale would be a farce. The "art" that Dr. Zull refers to is nothing less than encouraging desire or establishing values — one of the points of discussion in regards to our moral nature. He further explains what education looks like in the brain:

> Neuroscience has shown us two key things that lead to change in networks of neurons. The first one of these is simply practice. Neurons that fire a lot tend to form more connections and strengthen new connections. This is nothing new, of course, but it is more subtle than just drill, drill, drill.[210]

---

[208] Eagleman, *Brain*, 128.

[209] James Zull, "The Art of the Changing Brain," *Johns Hopkins University Online Journal*, http://education.jhu.edu/PD/newhorizons/Neurosciences/articles/The%20Art%20of%20the%20Changing%20Brain/.

[210] Ibid.

While Dr. Zull admits that neuroscience is not discovering any new secret to shaping the brain or neural functions — he stresses how repetition is key to learning. But he also notes that there is more to education than simply "drill, drill, drill." He later says,

> The other thing that helps neuron networks get stronger and become larger and more complex is emotion. There are recent experiments which show that such changes in networks can be generated simply by triggering neurons to dump "emotion chemicals" on the firing networks. These chemicals are things like adrenaline, serotonin, and dopamine, and they are delivered to specific parts of the brain by specific neuron pathways. Thus, the concomitant frequent firing and exposure to the chemicals of emotion lead to great change in neuronal networks. So the "art of changing the brain" comes down to some things that we have always known. *Practice and meaning are the most important parts of this art, but of course the student will not practice in a meaningful way unless she cares. Ultimately it is the learner that is in control.* The teacher can arrange the conditions and the challenges in ways that engage the learner, *but still we must have faith in learning itself* [emphasis added].[211]

That the student cares is another way of saying that an underlying desire necessary for learning has been realized in the student. Dr. Zull touches on humanity's dual nature by pointing out that there exist two parts of education: (1) the scientific or observable effects on the body, and (2) the spiritual reality including meaning, desire, faith, and emotion. Meaning, faith, and desire are key spiritual truths to both moral and academic education that can be fostered through repetition.

But there is also a converse side to neuroplasticity; if a person does not exercise or use his or her brain, then the brain will deteriorate and atrophy much like the body's muscles. Elizabeth Landau references Dr. Gupta's explanation:

> The flip side of plasticity is pruning. Brain areas can shrivel away if they are not being used. When it comes to using your limbs and other basic functions, it is basically a "use it or lose it" situation, Gupta said. If you don't use your right arm, for instance, the part of the brain corresponding to its usage will deteriorate. That's why

---

[211] Ibid.

rehabilitation to relearn how to move limbs and speak again is so important.[212]

Dr. Zull also remarks on the spiritual side of this process in discussing desire:

> Neurons have the ability to just stop firing when the stimulus turns out to be unimportant. This phenomenon is known as habituation, and it is the same thing that happens when we stop hearing the cars that go by our window on a busy street.[213]

When desire is absent or settings are no longer of value or of interest, then the brain responds by not "firing."[214] This reality exposes how important our desires and goals are both in maintaining a healthy brain and in education. Though our desires affect our physical nature, Scripture reveals desires or treasures to be sourced in the spiritual heart and not in the physical brain. Matthew 6:19-21 states,

---

[212] Sanjay Gupta quoted by Elizabeth Landau, "The Brain's Amazing Potential for Recovery," May 5, 2011, http://www.cnn.com/2011/HEALTH/05/05/ brain.plasticity.giffords/index.html.

[213] Zull, "Changing Brain."

[214] The nervous system similarly can atrophy as a side-effect to many psychotropic/neuroleptic medications that provide chemicals (often in excess), which are often normal products of the body. When the body realizes that it does not need to produce the chemicals that a given drug provides, the production of that chemical stops being made or is diminished. This is one reason why withdrawal from neuroleptics can be so dangerous; the body is not prepared for the sudden or even gradual removal of the substitute chemicals it has been depending upon. Dr. Peter Breggin explains, "While neuroleptic drugs are dangerous to take, they also are dangerous to stop taking too quickly. Disturbing muscular control problems can develop during the withdrawal period. Withdrawal can cause a temporary or permanent worsening of psychotic symptoms, with anxiety and even anguish, as a result of central nervous system rebound from the drugs" (Breggin, *Toxic Psychiatry*, 88).

> Do not lay up for yourselves treasures on earth, where moth and rust destroy and where thieves break in and steal, but lay up for yourselves treasures in heaven, where neither moth nor rust destroys and where thieves do not break in and steal. For where your treasure is, there your heart will be also.

When someone mentally desires something or judges stimuli to lack value, then the brain physically responds. Dr. Eagleman explains,

> Throughout our lives, our brains rewrite themselves to build dedicated circuitry for the *missions we practice* — whether that's walking, surfing, juggling, swimming, or driving [emphasis added]. This ability to burn programs into the structure of the brain is one of its most powerful tricks. It can solve the problem of complex movement using such little energy by wiring dedicated circuitry into the hardware. Once etched into the circuitry of the brain, these skills can be run without thinking.[215]

What we make to be our missions or desires require repetitive thoughts and actions that often form enduring and life-changing patterns known as habits, character, addictions, or if perceived as unwanted or impairing behavior by psychiatrists, as disorders.

While habits, such as tying a shoe, riding a bike, shooting a basketball, or speaking a foreign language, can certainly be formed so that thinking is not necessary, applied thinking is necessary to first form those habits. What is also interesting about such habits, though, is that neuroimaging reveals the brain to hardly be functioning when behavior is mastered. In other words, the more a task is practiced and mastery achieved, the less neural activity is needed to perform the task. Dr. Eagleman uses the current children's world record holder for cup-stacking, Austin Naber, to illustrate this point:

> In quick, fluid movements impossible to follow with your eyes, Austin transforms a stacked column of plastic cups into a symmetrical display of three separate pyramids. Then, with both hands dashing, he telescopes the pyramids back down into the two

---

[215] Eagleman, *Brain*, 81.

short columns, and then transmutes the columns into a single, tall pyramid, which is then collapsed into the original column of cups. He does this all in five seconds. I tried it, and it took me forty-three seconds on my best run. Watching Austin in action, you might expect his brain to be working overtime, burning an enormous amount of energy to coordinate these complex actions so quickly . . . As it turns out, the EEG result showed that my brain, not Austin's was the one working overtime, burning an enormous amount of energy to run this complex new task. My EEG showed high activity in the Beta wave frequency band, which is associated with extensive problem solving. Austin, on the other hand had high activity in the Alpha wave band, a state associated with the brain at rest. Despite the speed and complexity of his actions, Austin's brain was serene.[216]

Had neurologists not known Austin's history and level of mastery and had merely observed the results on his EEG, then they could have easily speculated that something was wrong in his brain. This illustrates that neuroscience — even in brain scans — cannot fully or even accurately always describe human realities through observation of the brain. It also raises an important question: if the brain goes into a "state of rest" during mastered activities, what then is controlling those activities and causing the body to do its amazing feats? Whatever the answer might be, two things are certain: (1) mental repetition that leads to habituation enables neuroplasticity to occur in healthy and damaged brains alike. (2) Desire and faith — both spiritual realities — continue to be prominent themes of discussion by professionals concerning human nature, behavior, and education.

Mental repetition

If neuroplasticity and normal education occur through mental repetition, it should be of no surprise then, to learn that God sets forth repetition — leading to habituation — as key to changing our minds and controlling our physical behavior. This reality is true for better or for worse. For example, the psalmist

---

[216] Ibid., 76-79.

writes in Psalm 119:11 that he hid (memorized) Scripture in his spiritual heart in order to behave in a specific way. The passage states, "I have stored up your word in my heart, that I might not sin against you." The spiritual activity of repetition in the mind or spiritual heart leads to direct control over purposeful or moral behavior. But to memorize or store up information in the spiritual heart requires both a desire to please God and mental repetition of that information.[217]

Not only does Scripture make the case that desire and repetition affect the human body and behavior, but so also do numerous secular studies. For example, London city cab drivers undergo some of the most rigorous and intense memorization through mental repetition. The prestigious occupation of driving a cab in London requires four years of intensive study. The arduous task of memorizing London's entire transportation system is considered by many to be one of the most difficult mental exercises known to man. The four years of intense study end in a test known as "the Knowledge of London"; if passed, it enables the student to become a "cabbie."[218]

While such a mental feat of learning the entire map of London is itself amazing — especially as many of the men who accomplish this task are uneducated, the physical results of such mental exercise are also interesting. Curiosity about how such

_____

[217] For further reading on the topics of repetition, desire, and memorization, see Daniel R. Berger II, *Teaching a Child to Pay Attention* (Taylors, SC: Alethia International Publishers, 2015).

[218] Jody Rosen, "The Knowledge, London's Legendary Taxi-Driver Test, Puts up a Fight in the Age of GPS," *New York Times*, November 10, 2014, http://www.nytimes.com/2014/11/10/t-magazine/london-taxi-test-knowledge.html?_r=0.

intense mental exercise affects the brain led neuroscientists to do studies which revealed

> visible differences in cabbie's brains: in the drivers, the posterior part of the hippocampus had grown physically larger than those in the control group-presumably causing their increased spatial memory. The researchers also found that the longer a cabbie has been doing his job, the bigger the change in that brain region, suggesting that the result was not simply reflecting a pre-existing condition of people who go into the profession, but instead resulted from practice. The cab-driver study demonstrates that adult brains are not fixed in place, but instead can reconfigure so much that the change is visible to the trained eye.[219]

Similarly, Jody Rosen explains,

> The brains of London taxi drivers have attracted scholarly attention. Eleanor Maguire, a neuroscientist at University College London, has spent 15 years studying cabbies and Knowledge boys. She has discovered that the posterior hippocampus, the area of the brain known to be important for memory, is bigger in London taxi drivers than in most people, and that a successful Knowledge candidate's posterior hippocampus enlarges as he progresses through the test. Maguire's work demonstrates that the brain is capable of structural change even in adulthood. The studies also provide a scientific explanation for the experiences of Knowledge students, the majority of whom have never pursued higher education and profess shock at the amount of information they are able to assimilate and retain.[220]

Neuroplasticity is a useful tool that can physically alter the brain even in uneducated adults. If the brain truly is the primary problem in mental issues, then repetition leading to habituation and positive changes in the brain and behavior would be the primary remedy doctors pursue. Neuroplasticity both changes behavior — as we observed in Psalm 119 — and it changes the physical structure of the brain to be healthier.

---

[219] Eagleman, *Brain*, 17-18.

[220] Rosen, "Age of GPS."

One note of warning, however, is needed. While some secularists — known as behaviorists[221] — propose that all humans need is repetition, Scripture does not focus on simply creating good habits, but forming right desires/motives that produce right thinking, emotions, behavior and eventually right habits. In other words, God is more concerned about people's spiritual heart and having a genuine relationship with His people than He is merely about physical behavior. Behaving a certain way should never be the ultimate goal; rather God desires a heart that seeks to know and please Him. When right desires and thoughts are in place, then right moral behaviors follow. Consequently, when right behaviors are repeated, then right habits can be formed and the brain can be strengthened. It is no wonder then, that Scripture consistently reveals this pattern of focusing on the heart with the anticipation of physical and behavioral changes (e.g., Proverbs 4: 20-27).[222] The discovery of the brain's neuroplasticity directly supports God's claim to have created mankind with both a moral and physical nature and places the brain-dysfunction theory into question.

---

[221] Gabrielle Weiss and Lily Trokenberg Hechtman, *Hyperactive Children Grown Up: ADHD in Children, Adolescents, and Adults*, 2nd ed. (New York: Guilford, 1993), 367.

[222] Daniel R. Berger II, *Teaching a Child to Pay Attention: Proverbs 4:20-27* (Taylors, SC: Alethia International Publications, 2015).

CHAPTER 7 – THE GENES' ABILITY TO CHANGE

Another medical field, which has emerged within the last thirty years and also undermines the unproven theory of brain-dysfunction and "genetic determinism,"[223] is the study of epigenetics. While this "new biology"[224] is founded on the reality of our psychosomatic nature, the research involved can still be twisted to fit the evolutionary idea of materialism. Nonetheless, many secular scientists and physicians have realized the dual nature of mankind through the scientific observations found in epigenetics. Former professor at Stanford University's School of Medicine, Bruce Lipton explains,

> Epigenetics, the study of the molecular mechanisms by which environment controls gene activity, is today one of the most active areas of scientific research. . . . I came to the conclusion that we are not victims of our genes, but master of our fates, able to create lives overflowing with peace, happiness, and love.[225]

This new science is exposing the determinism of evolutionary theory to simply be untrue. In other words, people have choices when it comes to moral issues of character, emotion, desire, and behavior and are not the victim of their brains, genes, or their environments. Dr. Lissa Rankin comments,

> Traditional genetic determinism, as elucidated by Watson and Crick, who discovered the DNA double helix, supports the notion that everything in the body is controlled by our genes—that essentially, our genes are our destiny. If this is true, we are literally victims of

---

[223] Lissa Rankin, *Mind over Medicine: Scientific Proof that You Can Heal Yourself* (New York: Hay House Inc., 2013), 25.

[224] Lipton, *Biology of Belief,* preface xxiv.

[225] Ibid., preface xxiv-v.

our genes. Heart disease, breast cancer, alcoholism, depression, high cholesterol—you name it. If it runs in your family, you're basically hosed. The dogma of genetic determinism, as it has been traditionally taught, is simple. You're born with your DNA, which then gets replicated as RNA before being translated into a protein. But the study of epigenetics is uncovering new theories that bring the whole notion of genetic determinism into question. . . . It's not as cut and dried as we once thought.[226]

Likewise, Dr. Lipton explains his own path to this discovery:

My final stop in conventional academia was at Stanford University's School of Medicine. By the time I was an unabashed proponent of a "new" biology, I had come to question not only Darwin's dog-eat-dog version of evolution but also biology's Central Dogma, the premise that genes control life. That scientific premise has one major flaw—genes cannot turn themselves on or off. In more scientific terms, genes are not "self-emergent." Something in the environment has to trigger gene activity. Though that fact had already been established by frontier science, conventional scientists blinded by genetic dogma had simply ignored it.[227]

Though Dr. Lipton notes that the theory of epigenetics undermines the deterministic view of brain-dysfunction based on scientific evidence, he fails in his statement to note that it is not simply environment that controls our body down to even the genes. Ultimately, the mind is seated above the brain, the body, and genetics.[228] In fact, epigenetics means "control above the genes."[229] Dr. Lissa Rankin explains,

So what's "above the genes" when we talk about epigenetics control? Yup. You guessed it; the mind. As it turns out, while you

---

[226] Rankin, *Mind over Medicine*, 25-26.

[227] Lipton, *Biology of Belief*, xxiv.

[228] This statement in no way neglects the reality that God sovereignly directs human life according to His will. It is made in reference to mankind alone.

[229] Lipton, *Biology of Belief*, 37.

can't change your DNA, you may be able to utilize the power of your mind to alter how your DNA expresses itself.[230]

Cognitive neuroscientist Caroline Leaf also emphasizes the mind's control over our genes:

> Thoughts collectively form your attitude, which is your state of mind, and it's your attitude and not your DNA that determines much of the quality of your life. This state of mind is a real, physical, electromagnetic, quantum, and chemical flow in the brain that switches groups of genes on or off in a positive or negative direction based on your choices and subsequent reactions. Scientifically, this is called epigenetics.[231]

Mental health advocates and researchers have long ignored the mind as separate from the brain. They have done so on the sole basis that accepting dualism does not fit into their evolutionary thinking and destroys their brain-dysfunction theory. But the evidence that the mind controls the physical nature is forcing their hand.

Genes, neurons, and the brain itself are not fixed as the brain-dysfunctionists propose. Dr. Lipton asserts,

> Genes-as-destiny theorists have obviously ignored hundred-year-old science about enucleated cells, but they cannot ignore new research that undermines their belief in genetic determinism. While the Human Genome Project was making headlines, a group of scientists were inaugurating a new, revolutionary field in biology called epigenetics. The science of *epigenetics*, which literally means "control above genetics," profoundly changes our understanding of how life is controlled. . . . Genes are not destiny![232]

Scientists now understand that the brain, genes, and the body all respond to how one thinks about life — whether adversely or

---

[230] Rankin, *Mind over Medicine*, 25.

[231] Leaf, *Switch on Your Brain*, 14.

[232] Lipton, *Biology of Belief*, 37.

positively.[233] Changing or morphing genes, chemical levels, or brain atrophy, though, are not the real problems but side-effects. Unfortunately, science can study only the visible effects, so many scientists focus only on the effects and ignore the true cause:

> Scientists have long been aware that our genes aren't chiseled in stone — they are in a constant dialogue with our environment. The epigenetic marking up of our DNA, discovered decades ago, is a key part of how that dialogue takes place. And while these marks are an important feature of our biology, the biggest flaw in many of the claims being made about epigenetics is that they confuse cause with effect.[234]

The author eventually notes that "epigenetic marks are a consequence of changes in the activity of our genes in response to our health, our environment, and our social experiences, but *they are not the underlying cause of those changes* [emphasis added]."[235] If anything, the study of epigenetics sheds light on the reality that the mind can and does alter and control the body. Likewise, these new scientific discoveries reveal that changes to genes are not the real problem; they are only a side-effect. This discovery leaves the genetic theory — proposed by determinists — to be a side-issue in discussions of causes and remedies to mental turmoil. Neuroscience can be helpful in understanding physical responses to mindsets, but God's Word provides the wisdom needed in spiritual issues of life and godliness to produce positive changes.

---

[233] Mark Ptashne, "Epigenics: Core Misconcept," *Proceedings of the National Academy of Sciences of the United States* 110, no. 18 (Apr 30, 2013): 7101-3, http://www.ncbi.nlm.nih.gov /pmc/articles/PMC3645541/.

[234] http://www.psmag.com/health-and-behavior/epigenetics-not-revolutionizing-biology.

[235] Ibid.

In fact, while the field of epigenetics is a relatively new scientific field, the idea of the mind sitting above the physical nature is well-established throughout Scripture. Granted, genes are not the focus of Scripture, but rather the mind's impact on the physical nature. For example, Proverbs 17:22 reveals that a joyful spiritual heart (mind) is medicine for those who are sad to the point of hopelessness: "A joyful heart is good medicine, but a crushed spirit [hopelessness or depression] dries up the bones." Not only is joy — a mental/spiritual reality — stated to be medicine, but the verse also claims that when joy is absent the human body is directly affected, a point that neuroscience is now realizing. In contrast to the secular construct of mental illness, Scripture clearly establishes that the spiritual nature of humanity controls what is morally carried out in the physical nature.

CHAPTER 8 – THE NERVOUS SYSTEM'S DESIGN

While the brain (and genetics) is typically the focus of study and theory within the secular construct of mental health, all of the senses and the nervous system are equally important in understanding the brain's function. Moreover, the nervous system and the five senses support the human psychosomatic nature and dispel the brain-dysfunction theory.

The Study of Psychonueroimmunology

An emerging field of science and medicine which, like the study of neuroplasticity and epigenetics, also undermines the current concept of mental illness is psychoneuroimmunology (PNI, also known as psychoneuroendocrinoimmunology or PNEI). Though virtually unknown by the general public, psychoneuroimmunology has amassed substantial evidence that is changing the way many professionals understand and approach humanity. For many clinicians the thought that the mind can control the brain, the nervous system, and the immune system is a novel idea. Yet, as we previously discussed, the anthropological position is a historical one (though not called PNI) that has been denied or ignored for too long. Nevertheless, PNI is now quickly gaining popularity among many medical professionals. Dr. Breggin comments, "A whole new field is developing, psychoneuroimmunology, based on the theory that our state of mind affects our brain, which in turn affects our immunological system."[236]

---

[236] Breggin, *Toxic Psychiatry*, 112.

Repeatable and validated discoveries conducted through PNI research undermine the belief in materialism and brain-based theories of man. Specifically, the field has discovered that the mind has executive control over many functions of the brain, the nervous system, and the immune system — thus the title *psychoneuroimmunology*.[237] Dr. Alan Watkins explains,

> It has been recognized for some time that mechanistic and materialistic ideas are insufficient to explain the human condition and the genesis of disease. . . . There is now a substantial amount of evidence from research into the mind (psychology), the brain (neurology) and the body's natural defenses (immunology) to suggest that the mind and body communicate with each other in a bidirectional flow of hormones, neuropeptides and cytokines.[238]

Materialist Dr. Daniel Stern testifies to the mind's importance in the foreword of Cozolino's *The Neuroscience of Psychotherapy*:

> Whatever the approach, lasting change in therapy occurs as a result of changes in the human mind . . . which involve changes in the functions of the brain. Exactly how the mind changes during the therapeutic process is the fundamental puzzle that the synthesis of neuroscience and psychotherapy seeks to solve.[239]

While it remains a mystery to those who hold to materialism — who limit their understanding to that which is observable, the mind's ability to directly affect the entire body is vital to most aspects of human life and especially to healing. Dr. Rankin offers insight into how faith can even heal the body of valid physical maladies as it controls the immune system:

---

[237] Sharon Begley, *Train Your Mind Change Your Brain* (New York: Ballantine Books, 2007). See also Jeffery Schwartz and Rebecca Gladding, *You Are Not Your Brain: The 4-Step Solution for Changing Bad Habits, Ending Unhealthy Thinking, and Taking Control of Your Life* (New York: Penguin Group, 2011), 36.

[238] Watkins, *Mind-Body Medicine*, 2.

[239] Louis Cozolino, *The Neuroscience of Psychotherapy: Building and Rebuilding the Human Brain*, (New York: W. W. Norton, 2002), preface ix.

> Positive belief and nurturing care may also alter the immune system. People treated with placebos may experience boosts in immune function which results from flipping off the stress response and initiating the relaxation response. Placebos may also suppress the immune system. . . . Positive belief and nurturing care may also decrease the body's acute phase response, a type of inflammatory response that lead to pain, swelling, fever, lethargy, apathy, and loss of appetite.[240]

Whether or not professionals wish to recognize that the mind (and faith) is essential to mental stability and physical healing, the evidence in scientific research is plentiful.

The field of PNI is not only being accepted as valid within physiological medicine, but also among many neurologists, psychiatrists, and other physicians concerning alleged mental illness. One psychiatrist who promotes the validity of PNI is Niall McLaren. He not only writes about the lack of evidence within the current construct and brain-dysfunction theory, he also dogmatically holds that the mind controls the executive moral functions of the brain:

> I have derived a formal model of mind based in a molecular resolution of the mind-brain problem. This leads to the concept of a cognitive psychiatry, where the thought processes drive brain activity, rather than the other way around, which is how biopsychiatry sees mental life. As a consequence, we can dramatically reduce drug use, admissions to hospital and the huge burden of mental disorder in the community. People who have previously been seen as invalids can take control of their lives and resume a productive and satisfying life without long-term psychiatric attention. All that remains now is to convince the mainstream of psychiatry that the direction they have been following for decades is not going to gain the benefits they hope. That is not likely to happen overnight.[241]

Because of his position, Dr. McLaren is obviously shunned by many neo-Kraepelinians and the pharmaceutical companies. But several others, such as Dr. Breggin, have realized the lack of evidence within biological psychiatry and have discovered how

---

[240] Rankin, *Mind over Medicine,* 12.

[241] Niall McLaren, http://www.niallmclaren.com/biography.html.

the mind is the executive of moral behavior and emotions.[242] Likewise, the American Psychology Association explains the power of the mind to heal the body:

> The past 15 years have seen an explosion of research findings from the fields of behavioral medicine and Psychoneuroimmunology demonstrating the effects of attitude, behavior, cognitive set, and unpleasant states of mind on psychology and illness. It is now accepted that such variables play a role in the course of diseases such as diabetes, heart disease, asthma, and cancer. Similarly, it is well established that these psychological factors can influence the pain experience, affect immune response, and have a demonstrable impact on health care variables like length of hospitalization, compliance with treatment, and response to surgery. Companion research also has shown, sometimes in dramatic and moving ways, how modifications of attitude, behavior, cognitive set, and unpleasant states of mind can promote healing.[243]

Former researcher for the NIH, Dr. Candace Pert also recognizes both the mind's reality and its influence on the physical nature:

> We can bring about the release of endorphins through our state of mind. . . . I like to think of mental phenomena as messengers bringing information and intelligence from the nonphysical world to the body, where they manifest via their physical substrate, the neuropeptides and their receptors.[244]

These physicians and scientific researchers explain the simple reality that our minds alter our physical nature. In truth, science reveals Descartes' idea that only the physical can affect the physical to be false. That the mind is the non-physical governor of morality and outworking emotions and behaviors must be considered.

What better facilitates understanding on how the mind affects the body is being able to take specific mental processes

---

[242] Breggin, *Toxic Psychiatry*, 112.

[243] Roger Greenberg, in *The Heart and Soul of Change: What Works in Therapy*, ed. Mark A. Hubble, Barry L. Duncan, and Scott D. Miller (Washington, D.C: American Psychological Association, 2005), 262-63.

[244] Pert, *Molecules of Emotion*, 311.

that Scripture deems to be moral and spiritual in nature and observe how these truths correspond with research being done on the brain, the nervous system, and the senses. For example, guilt and shame are two thought processes that are known to directly affect both the physical size of the brain as well as the rest of the body:

> Excessive guilt is a known symptom of adult depression [or is it sometimes the cause?], but a new study finds that such feelings in the childhood can predict future mental illness, including depression, anxiety, obsessive-compulsive disorder and bipolar disorder. . . . According to the researchers, children who displayed signs of pathological guilt had anterior insula with less volume.[245]

Though many secularists speculate that guilt is a symptom of mental illness, others realize that guilt is actually the cause of such emotions, mindsets, and behaviors that can even alter the physicality of the brain. In explaining why soldiers have post-traumatic stress, Dr. Grossman reveals that it is not the threat of dying or even danger that causes the most psychiatric stress: it is guilt.[246] After describing a horrific war scene, he writes,

> Strangely, such horrifying memories seem to have a much more profound effect on the combatant—the participant in battle—than the noncombatant, the correspondent, civilian, POW, or other passive observer of the battle zone. As we have seen, the combat soldier appears *to feel a deep sense of responsibility and accountability* for what he sees around him. It is as though every enemy dead is a human being he has killed, and every friendly dead is a comrade for whom he was responsible. With every effort to reconcile these two

---

[245] "Feelings of Guilt during Childhood Linked to Mental Illness," http://www.huffingtonpost.com/2015/01/07/guilt-mentalhealth_n_6423434.html? cps=gravity_2692_-376788313446572831. See also Andy C. Belden, et al., "Anterior Insula Volume and Guilt: Neurobehavioral Markers of Recurrence after Early Childhood Major Depressive Disorder," *JAMA Psychiatry* 72, no. 1 (January 2015): 40-48.

[246] Grossman, *On Killing*, 75.

responsibilities, *more guilt is added* to the horror that surrounds the soldier [emphasis added].[247]

Some secularists have even claimed that guilt causes mental illness because it physically alters the brain. Yet as Dr. Breggin points out, guilt is a mental exercise that exposes either a valid reason to perceive oneself as morally bad,[248] or as Dr. Whitfield notes, it is a deceptive thought that wrongly perceives responsibility when none exists.[249] In both possibilities, guilt is a moral exercise and a mental process of fear and self-judgment that directly affects the brain, emotions, behavior, and the health of the entire body. It is no wonder then that brain-dysfunction theorists desire to do away with the idea of guilt, since its existence reveals humanity's own understanding of human culpability.

But we must understand that guilt is the product of the moral nature of people whether or not it is justified—caused by either real culpability or from a false perception. Though guilt is not always justified and can sometimes be the product of the deceptive nature, Psalm 32:1-4 reveals that guilt is a common result of the spiritual human nature and that it affects everyone. Guilt restricts happiness and directly affects the physical existence. Verse 2 states, "Blessed is the one whose transgression is forgiven, whose sin is covered. Blessed is the man against whom the LORD counts no iniquity, and in whose spirit there is no deceit." Happiness is in part the result of dealing with guilt

---

[247] Ibid., 74. Grossman goes on to write that "you don't even have to personally kill to experience these response stages and the interaction between the exhilaration and remorse stages" (246).

[248] Breggin, *Toxic Psychiatry*, 222.

[249] Whitfield, *Truth about Mental Illness*, 16.

and sin. But man can only deal with his guilt and deceptive nature through accepting the guilt offering of Jesus Christ (Jeremiah 30:15).

It is no surprise that secular studies are now beginning to realize the correlation between guilt and depression. Dr. Andy Belden et al. explains,

> To date, one of the most consistent and robust correlates of PO depression has been the tendency for pathological guilt. This includes both the experience of excessive guilt and infrequent or chronic maladaptive attempts to repair, amend, or correct wrongdoings (real or imagined) from which a sense of guilt emerged.[250]

The reality of guilt affecting the spiritual nature of mankind is widely understood.

But according to Scripture, guilt also alters the body. Verses 3-4 state, "For when I kept silent, my bones wasted away through my groaning all day long. For day and night your hand was heavy upon me; my strength was dried up as by the heat of summer. Selah" Although God's wisdom has declared that man's guilt negatively affects his physical nature long before neuroimaging was available, neurological research is now offering a similar perspective:

> Findings from disparate but highly related areas of social, affective, and clinical neuroscience provide empirical support for our hypothesis that preschool depression would predict Anterior Insula (AI) volume reduction when measured at school age and that the early experience of pathological guilt may be an important symptom in the expected relationship between Preschool-onset Major Depressive Disorder and reduced AI volumes.[251]

As with all conclusions about the mind, Dr. Belden's conclusions about his findings are based upon faith. But these types of

---

[250] Belden, et al., "Anterior Insula Volume and Guilt," 40-48; Also available from http://archpsyc.jamanetwork.com/article.aspx? articleid=1935483.

[251] Ibid.

studies offer observable evidence that the spiritual nature (guilt in this case) directly affects and alters the physical, including the brain.

Guilt is not a scientific concept or a byproduct of the involuntary nervous system; rather guilt is the byproduct of the voluntary or moral nature of man,[252] which explains why guilt and the guilt offering of Christ are discussed at great length in Scripture and why secular proponents of determinism/materialism want to eliminate it, excuse it, and diminish its cause.[253]

Like Jeremiah 17:9, Psalm 32:2b-4 also shows that deception impacts our spiritual and physical natures:

> Blessed is the man . . . in whose spirit there is no deceit. For when I kept silent, my bones wasted away through my groaning all day long. For day and night your hand was heavy upon me; my strength was dried up as by the heat of summer.

While the brain is most often blamed as the greatest problem in mental struggles, some secularists recognize that our natural deception and inability to deal with our own sense of morality (sinful nature) are the true sources of our greatest mental pain. Dr. Bessel van der Kolk remembers that his professor of psychiatry at Harvard, the late Elvin Semrad, encouraged his students to be completely honest with themselves: "The greatest sources of our suffering are the lies we tell ourselves."[254] Scripture, however, has been testifying of this reality well before Semrad's assertion.

---

[252] Satel and Lilienfeld, *Brainwashed*, 96.

[253] Richard Dawkins, "Let's All Stop Beating Basil's Car," http://edge.org/q2006/q06_9.html.

[254] Van der Kolk, *Body Keeps the Score*, 26-27.

As with guilt and deception, stress can also alter the brain's physicality.[255] In 2014 neuroscientists at the University of California conducted studies which they claim reveal this truth:

> Neuroscientists have discovered how chronic stress and cortisol can damage the brain. A new study reconfirms the importance of maintaining healthy brain structure and connectivity by reducing chronic stress. Neuroscientists at the University of California, Berkeley, have found that chronic stress triggers long-term changes in brain structure and function. Their findings might explain why young people who are exposed to chronic stress early in life are prone to mental problems such as anxiety and mood disorders later in life, as well as learning difficulties. . . . "We studied only one part of the brain, the hippocampus, but our findings could provide insight into how white matter is changing in conditions such as schizophrenia, autism, depression, suicide, ADHD and PTSD," Kaufer said. The hippocampus regulates memory and emotions, and plays a role in various emotional disorders and has been known to shrink under extended periods of acute stress.[256]

Such descriptive studies allow secularists to conclude that stress causes mental illness and to assert their construct as valid. Similar studies, however, also reveal that such physical alterations to the brain can be reversed through empathy, rhetoric, and repetition, and that the brain can be restored to its original physical properties.[257] In other words, neuroplasticity can occur. So stress is not actually the cause of alternations in the brain, but it is how one thinks about or perceives such a situation and then reacts to it that determines physical changes. Once again, the mind — its perceptions — has great power over the physical brain. Dr. Alan Watkins comments,

> There is an enormous amount of research characterizing the physiological response to stress. Stressful situations are known to activate central autonomic nuclei and the sympathetic adreno-medullary (SAM) axis, in addition to the HPAC axis. These two

---

[255] The topic of stress will be discussed further in the next volume.

[256] http://www.psychologytoday.com/blog/the-athletes-way/201402/chronic-stress-can-damage-brain-structure-and-connectivity.

[257] Ibid.

pathways underpin different behavioral responses, and are associated with different emotional moods.[258]

Again, it is not actually the stress, however, that is responsible for the physical changes, but one's "responses" to the stress causes the body's reactions. Different people think differently about the same life events, and so their physical responses likewise vary. This variety in reactions is due in great part to different perceptions of life or worldviews. Dr. Lipton explains,

> Our responses to environmental stimuli are indeed controlled by perceptions, but not all of our learned perceptions are accurate. Not all snakes are dangerous! Yes, perception "controls" biology, but as we've seen, these perceptions can be true or false. Therefore, we would be more accurate to refer to these controlling perceptions as beliefs. Beliefs control biology.[259]

Our beliefs or perceptions about our experiences directly affect our physical nature. If we rely on our deceptive natures to perceive life, we will inevitably react accordingly and destructively.

As with guilt, deception, and stress, hope is a mindset that directly affects both the physical and spiritual natures. The American Psychological Association comments,

> The loss of hope—hopelessness—has been associated with health complications and poor treatment outcomes. For example, hopelessness has been related to greater tumor progression and earlier death among cancer patients, and to increased morbidity and mortality from ischemic heart disease. In a related study, Oxman, Freeman, and Manheimer (1995) examined the relationship between response to cardiac surgery and religious conviction, recognizing the powerful experience of hope and optimism that religious faith affords patients confronting serious illness.[260]

---

[258] Watkins, *Mind-Body Medicine*, 11.

[259] Lipton, *Biology of Belief*, 105.

[260] Hubble, Duncan, and Miller, *Heart and Soul of Change*, 267.

Hope is even a key characteristic of the psychiatric disorders of depression and bipolar. But hope is never disconnected from faith (Hebrews 11:1-3).

The field of psychoneuroimmunology reveals that how one thinks affects both the brain and the immune system. Having negative thoughts such as guilt, stress, or hopelessness without properly dealing with them often leads to valid physical impairment.[261] Likewise, thinking positively, forming mindsets that please God, and wisely dealing with deception and guilt can provide man with physical health. The brain is certainly involved in human behavior, but the mind is the executive over moral actions.

The Dual Nature of the Nervous System

Though believed to be only physiological in nature, the nervous system offers compelling evidence for dualism. In fact, it is widely accepted as scientifically sound that the nature of the nervous system is dualistic: there exists both a mentally controlled or volitional aspect of the nervous system and a brain-based autonomic or automatic function of the nervous system, which occurs without willpower or mental thought. An example of the autonomic or involuntary functions of the brain and nervous system can be seen in the brain's ability to regulate "heart rate, blood pressure, digestion, and bladder function."[262] In contrast, the mind must instruct the brain to communicate with the hand to reach out and take an object from a shelf, to punch someone in the face, or to steal. The hand will not

---

[261] Normal human reactions will be discussed further in the next volume.

[262] "Peripheral Neuropathy: Potentially Disabling Nerve Problems," *Mayo Clinic Health Letter* 29, no. 10 (October 2011): 2.

automatically behave in this moral way unless there is a willful intention or purpose established by the mind and carried out in the brain, the nervous system, and the rest of the physiology. Such a reality reveals alleged mental illnesses, such as kleptomania,[263] and theories of moral "executive function"[264] to be false.

Though discussed earlier, it is worth noting again: the Bible teaches that behavior carried out with purpose, intention, or desire is moral in nature. Colossians 3:17 and 23 state, "And whatever you do, in word or deed, do everything in the name of the Lord Jesus, giving thanks to God the Father through him . . . Whatever you do, work heartily, as for the Lord and not for men." Similarly, 1 Corinthians 10:31 echoes this sentiment: "So, whether you eat or drink, or whatever you do, do all to the glory of God." Paul reveals that our minds or spiritual hearts produce intentional behavior.

People engage in two types of behavior, which reflect the two natures of the nervous system. We can mentally choose behavior, and we automatically behave in amoral ways by means of our brains, nervous systems, and senses. While still holding to evolutionary belief, Dr. Pert notes the psychosomatic nature of the five senses:

---

[263] "Kleptomania (klep-toe-MAY-nee-uh) is the recurrent failure to resist urges to steal items that you generally don't really need and that usually have little value. Kleptomania is a serious mental health disorder that can cause much emotional pain to you and your loved ones if not treated" (http://www.mayoclinic.org/diseases-conditions/kleptomania/basics/definition/con-20033010).

[264] Sheik Hosenbocus and Raj Chahal, "A Review of Executive Function Deficits and Pharmacological Management in Children and Adolescents," *Journal of the Canadian Academy of Child and Adolescent Psychiatry* 21, no. 3 (2012): 223–29.

> We have found that in virtually all locations where information from any of the five senses — sight, sound, taste, smell, and touch — enters the nervous system, we will find a high concentration of neuropeptides receptors. We have termed these regions "nodal points" to emphasize that they are places where a great deal of information converges. . . . These nodal points *seem to be designed* so that they can be accessed and modulated by almost all neuropeptides as they go about their job of processing information, prioritizing it, and biasing it to cause unique neurophysiological changes. . . . *Emotions and bodily sensations are thus intricately intertwined, in a bidirectional network in which each can alter the other.* Usually this process takes place at an unconscious level, but it can also surface into consciousness under certain conditions, or be brought into consciousness by *intention* [emphases added].[265]

As we have noted, intention or purpose indicates morals and mental process. Surprisingly, Pert also states that the senses were "designed" to function in a "bodymind" or dualistic manner. Such language casts doubt on the traditional evolutionary view of the human body. Combining her key phrases, we can understand why the senses "seem to be designed" "in a psychosomatic network."[266] Pert attempts to explain how the spiritual and physical natures merge using scientific lingo, but her statements direct the reader more toward faith and religion than they do science.

Though it is convenient for secularists to promote the idea that the brain is responsible for every unwanted or impairing moral behavior, Scripture points to a person's will or depraved nature in moral matters. Paul even references the "law of sin" in Romans 7:21-8:4 to show that that people are not products of bio-determinism, but of meaningful choice. Unfortunately, without Christ, as Paul explains further in Romans and as we observed in Galatians 5, the default position of all humanity is to reject God's righteousness and choose foolish mindsets and behavior.

---

[265] Pert, *Molecules of Emotion,* 142.

[266] Ibid., 143.

In addition to the clarity of the Scripture on this point, many secularists also see the voluntary and involuntary realities of the nervous system as showing our dualistic nature. Secular psychiatrist, Thomas Szasz writes,

> Just as laypersons distinguish between voluntary actions and involuntary movements, so anatomists and physiologists distinguish between the voluntary nervous system and the involuntary nervous system. The concepts of voluntary-involuntary are indispensable for the formation of moral judgments and the administration of the law, as well as for the distinction between malingering as voluntary action and disease as involuntary happening.[267]

Szasz' remarks express our full responsibility for that which is voluntary and leaves us unable to blame such moral actions on physical disease.

The mind's responsibility to control the moral nature can be better understood by its ability to control even the autonomic functions of the body. When it comes to autonomic/amoral functions of the body — such as breathing, sleeping, swallowing, and blinking — the brain is the primary governor, and no involvement of the moral mind is needed. Though mental function is not necessary, the mind can actually override many of the brain's autonomic functions. For example, the brain commands the eyes to blink, the lungs to breathe, and the heart to beat, yet one can blink the eyes as desired, swallow at will and even stop breathing for a brief time or take deeper breaths. These behaviors reveal that the moral mind can behave intentionally even in the involuntary functions of the body. Dr. van der Kolk explains,

> There is a simple way to experience these two [nervous] systems for yourself. Whenever you take a deep breath, you activate the SNS [the sympathetic nervous system; one part of the autonomic nervous system]. The resulting burst of adrenaline speeds up your heart,

---

[267] Thomas Szasz, *Psychiatry: The Science of Lies* (New York: Syracuse University Press, 2008), 36.

which explains why many athletes take a few short, deep breaths before starting competition.[268]

To understand this mind-brain connection more fully, however, we must look specifically at the five senses, which are directly connected to the nervous system. Scripture, in fact, regularly discusses our senses as vital for functioning both physically and spiritually.

One of the most complex senses that involves almost every part of the brain is the sense of vision.[269] It is widely understood that sight is physical in nature, but Scripture claims it to be a spiritual activity as well. Matthew 5:28 says, "But I say to you that everyone who looks at a woman with lustful intent has already committed adultery with her in his heart." Such an understanding presents the sense of sight as not merely being an activity of the brain, but an activity of the spiritual heart, imagination, or mind done with intention. Similarly, Job 31:1 ff. presents sight as a behavior occurring from the willful purpose of the mind or spiritual heart. The text states, "I have made a covenant with my eyes; how then could I gaze at a virgin?" Seeing is an intentional spiritual behavior that is carried out in the physical body. Science can certainly study the brain and eyes' involvement with vision, but science is unable to study the motivation and willful mental process also involved in the sense of sight.

To understand just how involved the mind is in the senses, one only needs to study hallucinations. Although we will discuss hallucinations as they relate to the secular idea of

---

[268] Van der Kolk, *Body Keeps the Score*, 77.

[269] Ramachandran and Blakeslee, *Phantoms in the Brain*, 69-75; 88-112. See also Candace B. Pert, *Molecules of Emotion: The Science behind Mind-Body Medicine* (New York: Scribner, 1997), 142-43.

psychosis and the construct of schizophrenia in particular in the next volume, we must note that all five senses can and often do produce hallucinations. In fact, studies in sensory deprivation reveal that when sensory stimuli are absent (in sensory deprivation studies they are denied), hallucinations are the normal response. Neurologist Oliver Sacks explains this phenomenon in reference to the eyes and the studies done by blindfolding healthy people:

> The blindfolds, which allowed the subjects to close or move their eyes, were worn continuously for ninety-six hours. Ten of the thirteen subjects experienced hallucinations, sometimes during the first hours of blindfolding, but always by the second day, whether their eyes were open or not. Typically the hallucinations would appear suddenly and spontaneously, then disappear just as suddenly after seconds or minutes. . . . The subjects reported a range from simple hallucinations (flashing lights, phosphenes, geometrical patterns) to complex ones (figures, faces, hands, animals, buildings, and landscapes).[270]

Similarly, Dr. Eagleman remarks,

> In the traditional model of vision, perception results from a procession of data that begins from the eyes and end with some mysterious end point in the brain. But despite the simplicity of that assembly-line model of vision, it's incorrect. In fact, the brain generates its own reality, even before it receives information coming in from the eyes and the other senses. This is known as the internal model.[271]

While brain-dysfunctionists naturally blame *internal model* on the brain, "generating its own reality" can just as easily be attributed to the mind/imagination. The mind fills in its need for sensory stimulation when none exists. This sensory phenomenon can also be observed in Charles Bonnet Syndrome, a syndrome that affects millions of people and is the direct result of eye injury or

---

[270] Sacks, *Hallucinations*, 38-39.

[271] Eagleman, *Brain*, 51.

visual processing impairment and where hallucinations are one of the key side effects.[272]

Many secularists assert or at least imply that the senses also consist of physical and non-physical realities. German physicist, often called the founding father of visual science, Hermann von Helmholtz called perception an "unconscious inference."[273] After years of research, he concluded that the human body and the mind work together to make assumptions and inferences about what is being seen rather than always seeing an accurate reality. In other words, both a person's imagination and real visual images merge to form what he/she believes that they see. Dr Ramachandran also remarks about visual perception:

> Every act of perception, even something as simple as viewing a drawing of a cube, involves an act of *judgment* by the brain. In making these *judgments*, the brain takes advantage of the fact that the world we live in is not chaotic and amorphous; it has stable physical properties. During evolution—and partly during childhood as a result of learning—these stable properties become incorporated into the visual areas of the brain as certain "assumptions" or *hidden knowledge* about the world that can be used to eliminate ambiguity in perception.[274]

Dr. Ramachandran attributes the work of the imagination to the brain, but within materialistic thinking the brain and the mind are one. Human imagination (the mind's ability to produce non-physical images and ideas) represents another spiritual aspect of our heart and spiritual senses that is directly connected to the act of seeing. Dr. Ramachandran further explains,

> What is visual imagination? Are the same parts of your brain active when you imagine an object—say, a cat—as when you look at it

[272] Ramachandran and Blakeslee, *Phantoms in the Brain*, 106.

[273] E. Bruce Goldstein, ed., *Cognitive Psychology: Connecting Mind, Research and Everyday Experience*, 3rd ed. (Belmont, CA: Wadsworth, 2011), 63.

[274] Ramachandran and Blakeslee, *Phantoms in the Brain*, 67-68.

actually sitting in front of you? A decade ago, these might have been considered philosophical questions, but recently cognitive scientists have begun to probe these processes at the level of the brain itself and have come up with some surprising answers. It turns out that the human visual system has an astonishing ability to make educated guesses based on the fragmentary and evanescent images dancing in the eyeballs. . . . Vision involves a great deal more than simply transmitting an image to a screen in the brain and that it is an active, constructive process. A specific manifestation of this is the brain's remarkable capacity for dealing with inexplicable gaps in the visual image—a process that is sometimes loosely referred to as "filling in."[275]

Likewise, Dr. Eagleman remarks, "Your brain collects up all the information from the senses before it decides upon a story of what happens."[276] But is it the brain or the mind that truly forms perception? The answer depends upon whether you are a materialistic or a dualist. Genesis 6:5 states, "And GOD saw that the wickedness of man was great in the earth, and that every imagination of the thoughts of his heart was only evil continually (KJV)." Man's spiritual intentions—imagination or spiritual sight—guide not only his eyes, but his entire life. Likewise, in Luke 11:34-35, Luke the physician states, "Your eye is the lamp of your body. When your eye is healthy, your whole body is full of light, but when it is bad, your body is full of darkness. Therefore be careful lest the light in you be darkness." Luke is speaking here of vision-both morally and physically; the two are often not separated (Matthew 6:22-23). Some neuroscientists even believe that dreams, which occur during the rapid eye movement phase of sleep (REM),[277] illustrate the non-physical connection of the imagination (they often call the imagination "suppressed memories" or the "subconscious") and

---

[275] Ramachandran and Blakeslee, *Phantoms in the Brain,* 88.

[276] Eagleman, *Brain,* 49.

[277] Sacks, *Hallucinations,* 225-26.

132

the physical eye.[278] The sense of vision is a combination of both spiritual and physical and reflects the spiritual nature of the Creator (1 Chronicles 28:9).

As with vision, hearing and tasting are carried out in both of our natures. Proverbs 16:24 states, "Gracious words are like a honeycomb, sweetness to the soul and health to the body." This passage not only specifically states the dualistic nature of humanity (using the terms "soul" and "body"), it also points out that our senses are physical as well as directly connected to our spiritual nature. Gracious words are sweet to the soul and health to the body; they directly affect the non-material soul and the physical body. Here the spiritual (that which is real but unseen) directly alters the physical.[279] But if we understand that the entire physical world was created by words, then this truth makes even more sense. Hebrews 11:3 states, "By faith we understand that the universe was created by the word of God, so that what is seen was not made out of things that are visible."

Like the senses of sight and taste, the sense of hearing is mentioned as affecting the physical and spiritual natures. Proverbs 16:24 states that gracious words are sweet to the soul and health to the body. But it is not just the Bible that reveals words to be powerful enough to alter the physiology of the brain; secular research also reveals the same: "We now recognize that certain psychotherapies can modify the executive functions

---

[278] Dr. Ramachandran proposes another theory based upon clinical observation of the direct correlation of Rapid Eye Movement (REM) during sleep and memories or thoughts in the form of dreams occurring at the same time (V.S. Ramachandran and Sandra Blakeslee, *Phantoms in the Brain: Probing the Mysteries of the Human Mind* [New York: William Morrow and Company, 1998], 147).

[279] Honey directly affects the non-material soul and the physical body as it is pleasurable as well as healthy.

of the brain concentrated primarily in frontal lobe areas, the precise factors that promote such changes remain ambiguous."[280] The mystery of this phenomenon can be understood only by accepting the dual nature of mankind.

In Romans 10:17, hearing is said to also enable the spiritual process of faith. In Ephesians 2:8, saving faith is shown to be a gift of God — a spiritual reality — not something anyone can produce independently. Yet secularists have tried — but to no avail — to locate where faith is produced within the brain. For example, Dr. Ramachandran speculates,

> Could it be that human beings have actually evolved specialized neural circuitry for the sole purpose of mediating religious experience? The human belief in the supernatural is so widespread in all societies all over the world that it's tempting to ask whether the propensity for such beliefs might have a biological basis. If so, you'd have to answer a key question: What sorts of Darwinian selection pressures could lead to such a mechanism? And is there such a mechanism; is there a gene or set of genes concerned mainly with religiosity and spiritual leanings?[281]

While secularists attempt to solve these mysteries within their theory, the dualistic approach found in Scripture has already revealed that it is hearing — both a physical and spiritual exercise — that enables faith.

Human communication is both spiritual and physical. Proverbs 12:18 offers one example of the dual nature of communication: "There is one whose rash words are like sword thrusts, but the tongue of the wise brings healing." Or take for example the father's words to his son in Proverbs: "My son, be attentive to my words; incline your ear to my sayings. Let them not escape from your sight; keep them within your heart. For they are life to those who find them, and healing to all their flesh

---

[280] Panksepp, *Biological Psychiatry*, 10.

[281] Ramachandran and Blakeslee, *Phantoms in the Brain*, 183.

(4:20-22)." All of these passages reflect that gracious words —
God's wisdom — bring spiritual and physical healing to those
willing to receive them.

The sense of touch to affect both the physical and spiritual
natures is surprisingly powerful. Although there are numerous
passages in Scripture which present the moral and physical
nature of touch (e.g., 1 Corinthians 6:9-10), research is revealing
similar findings. The importance of physical touch can be
observed in the mother-infant relationship. Daniel Goleman
explains,

> The experience of being touched, new research shows, has direct and
> crucial effects on the *growth of the body as well as the mind* [emphasis
> added]. Touch is a means of communication so critical that its
> absence retards growth in infants, according to researchers who are
> for the first time determining the neurochemical effects of skin-to-
> skin contact. The new work focuses on the importance of touch itself,
> not merely as part of, say, a parent's loving presence. The findings
> may help explain the long-noted syndrome in which infants [282]
> deprived of direct human contact grow slowly and even die.

But the parents benefit from skin-to-skin contact as well.
Katherine Harmon comments,

> It seems to help the mothers, too. It reduces their stress level — they
> report lower levels of depression, they seem to be able to be more
> sensitive to their baby's cues and the babies are more responsive to
> the mother through the whole first three months. They're
> recognizing their mother earlier, so the relationship between the
> mother and baby is off to a facilitated start. It works the same way [283]
> with fathers, too.

It is not just the parent-infant relationship that benefits though:
scientists are quickly realizing that touch is more than a physical
experience: "We used to think that touch only served to intensify

---

[282] Daniel Goleman, "The Experience of Touch: Research Points to a Critical
Role," *New York Times*, February 2, 1988.

[283] Katherine Harmon, "How Important is Physical Contact with Your
Infant?" *Scientific America*, May 6, 2010, http://www.scientificamerican.com/
article/infant-touch/.

communicated emotions," Dr. Hertenstein said. Now it turns out to be "a much more differentiated signaling system than we had imagined."[284] Others note that touch can ease pain, lift the spirits of those who are considered depressed, and even encourage faith in positive outcomes.[285] Maia Szalavitz writes,

> The evidence that such messages can lead to clear, *almost immediate changes in how people think and behave is accumulating fast* [emphasis added]. Students who received a supportive touch on the back or arm from a teacher were nearly twice as likely to volunteer in class as those who did not, studies have found. A sympathetic touch from a doctor leaves people with the impression that the visit lasted twice as long, compared with estimates from people who were untouched. Research by Tiffany Field of the Touch Research Institute in Miami has found that a massage from a loved one can not only ease pain but also soothe depression and strengthen a relationship.[286]

Clearly human touch affects both our physical and spiritual natures.

Not only is research in neuroscience revealing the power of touch to aid in healing and affect the physical and mental realities, but scientific studies are also exposing a seemingly unexplainable non-physical reality of the sense of touch. Phantom limbs offer insight into the psychosomatic nature. After explaining how the brain remaps itself (neuroplasticity), Dr. Ramachandran concedes that neuroplasticity alone cannot explain genuine pain and sensations experienced by amputees. He states,

---

[284] Benedict Carey, "Evidence That Little Touches Do Mean So Much," *New York Times*, February 22, 2010, http://www.nytimes.com/2010/02/23/health/23mind.html?scp=3&sq=touch&st= cse&_r=0.

[285] Maia Szalavitz, "Touching Empathy: Lack of Physical Affection Can Actually Kill Babies," *Psychology Today*, March 1, 2010, https://www.psychologytoday.com /blog/born-love/201003/touching-empathy.

[286] Benedict Carey, "Evidence That Little Touches Do Mean So Much."

But this cannot be the whole story. First, it doesn't explain why so many people with phantoms claim that they can move their "imaginary" limbs voluntarily. What is the source of this illusion of movement? Second, it doesn't explain the fact that these patients sometimes experience intense agony in the missing limb, the phenomenon called phantom pain. Third, what about a person who is born without an arm? Does remapping also occur in his brain, or does the hand area of the cortex simply never develop because he never had an arm? Would he experience a phantom? Can someone be born with phantom limbs? The idea seems preposterous, but if there's one thing I've learned over the years it's that neurology is full of surprises.[287]

Dr. Ramachandran goes on to share a story about a girl named Mirabelle who was born without arms yet experiences vivid phantom sensations.[288] He concludes from the story of Mirabelle (and others) that "each of us has an internally hard-wired image of the body and limbs at birth — an image that can survive indefinitely, even in the face of contradictory information from the senses."[289] Neurologist Oliver Sacks also remarks of the nature of phantom limbs:

Phantom limbs are hallucinations insofar as they are *perceptions of something that has no existence in the outside world*, but they are not quite comparable to hallucinations of sight and sound. . . . They are felt as an integral part of one's own body, unlike any other sort of hallucination. Finally, while visual hallucinations such as those of Charles Bonnet syndrome are varied and full of invention [imagination], a phantom closely resembles the physical limb that was amputated in size and shape. A phantom foot may have a bunion, if the real one did; a phantom arm may wear a wristwatch, if the real arm did. In this sense, a phantom is more like a memory than an invention.[290]

Like Dr. Ramachandran, Dr. Sacks concludes that the keen awareness of still having limbs when no physical limb exists is normal and universal. He states,

---

[287] Ramachandran and Blakeslee, *Phantoms in the Brain*, 40-42.

[288] Ibid.

[289] Ibid., 42.

[290] Sacks, *Hallucinations*, 276-77.

> The near universality of phantom limbs after amputation, the immediacy of their appearance, and their identity with the corporeal limbs in whose stead they appear suggest that, in some sense, they are already in place—revealed, so to speak, by the act of amputation. . . . The feeling of a limb as a sensory and motor part of oneself seems to be innate, built-in, hardwired—and this supposition is supported by the fact that people born without limbs may nonetheless have vivid phantoms in their place.[291]

In similar fashion, neurologist Silas Weir Mitchell stated in 1872 that "nearly every man who loses a limb carries about with him a constant or inconstant phantom of the missing member, a sensory ghost of that much of himself."[292] Phantom limbs help illuminate the reality that our senses and nervous system are not merely physical in nature; they are psychosomatic or have a "sensory ghost." When we think of pain, it is both a physical occurrence and a spiritual one, even when the physical reality of the sense is removed.[293]

If pain is spiritual—a product of the fall—then those who are not redeemed will feel pain in eternity.[294] This is precisely what Scripture presents to be true. Whereas for believers, death, sorrow, and pain will be taken away (Revelations 21:4), Luke 16:19-24 claims that taste, feeling, hearing, sight, thought, speaking, and pain are all present in Hell:

> There was a rich man who was clothed in purple and fine linen and who feasted sumptuously every day. And at his gate was laid a poor man named Lazarus, covered with sores, who desired to be fed with what fell from the rich man's table. Moreover, even the dogs came and licked his sores. The poor man died and was carried by the angels to Abraham's side. The rich man also died and was buried,

---

[291] Ibid., 277.

[292] Silas Weir Mitchell, *Injuries of Nerves and their Consequences* (Philadelphia: Lippincott: 1872).

[293] Eagleman, *Brain,* 49.

[294] For those who are redeemed, sorrow, pain, and death will end with Jesus' return (Revelation 21:4).

and in Hades, being in torment, he lifted up his eyes and saw Abraham far off and Lazarus at his side. [24] And he called out, "Father Abraham, have mercy on me, and send Lazarus to dip the end of his finger in water and cool my tongue, for I am in anguish in this flame."

The existence of the senses in eternity is scripturally based. Such a reality also exposes that the physical senses are not disconnected from man's spiritual nature.

Many neurologists and neuroscientists realize that sensory perception/experiences are more than simply bodily phenomenon. For example, Dr. Ramachandran and others suggest that pain is a mental illusion rather than a physical reality.[295] While we may disagree that pain is merely an illusion, his statement reflects that pain is sensed both physically and spiritually. It is no wonder then, that neurologists describe phantom limbs as "a portion of body image which is lost or dissociated from its natural extraneous, it may be intrusive or deceptive."[296]

In regards to the senses and phantom limbs, it is important to mention that they not only expose humanity's dual nature, but they also reveal that all people have a voluntary and moral will. For example, Dr. Ramachandran states, "When you decide to move your hand, the chain of events leading to its movements originate in the frontal lobes,"[297] and Dr. Sacks says,

The most fundamental difference between phantom limbs and other hallucinations is that they can be moved voluntarily, whereas visual

---

[295] Ramachandran and Blakeslee, *Phantoms in the Brain*, 54-55.

[296] Sacks, *Hallucinations*, 279.

[297] Ramachandran and Blakeslee, *Phantoms in the Brain*, 44.

> and auditory hallucinations proceed autonomously, outside one's control. . . . A phantom limb is capable of phantom action.[298]

Likewise, others such as Dr. William James believed that "the fundamental questions" concerning phantom limbs are "will" and "effort."[299]

In spite of these facts, secularists propose that only physical elements can control the physical faculties.[300] Though this philosophy is widespread in the secular scientific community, it ignores or rejects the spiritual influence of the mind on the brain and the dual nature of the nervous system.

---

[298] Sacks, *Hallucinations*, 278.

[299] Quoted by Oliver Sacks, *Hallucinations*, 276.

[300] Begley, *Train Your Mind*, 133.

CHAPTER 9 – FAITH'S INFLUENCE IN HEALING

Though western medicine typically refrains from considering faith as influential (even necessary) in healing, recent studies reveal that faith is still the most relevant corollary for mental stability and often even for physical health. One of the greatest evidences of faith's importance is what is known in science and medicine alike as the placebo effect. Many people are familiar with the placebo effect as being only a sugar pill that is presented as being genuine medicine and producing genuine change but without chemicals in the pill whereby change can be attributed to the physical medicine. Dr. Bruce Lipton explains,

> Every medical student learns, at least in passing, that the mind can affect the body. They learn that some people get better when they believe (falsely) they are getting medicine. When patients get better by ingesting a sugar pill, medicine defines it as the placebo effect.[301]

The placebo effect, however, is not only observed within pharmacology,[302] but it also affects every facet of treatment in both spiritual and physical matters to the point that it can change the biochemistry of patients. Dr. Lissa Rankin explains,

> When given placebos, bald men grow hair, blood pressure drops, warts disappear, ulcers heal, stomach acid levels decrease, colon inflammation decreases, cholesterol levels drop, jaw muscles relax and swelling goes down after dental procedures, brain dopamine levels increase in patients with Parkinson's disease, white blood cell activity increases, and the brains of people who experience pain relief light up on imaging studies. These findings convinced me. Placebos don't just change how you feel, they change your biochemistry. This is where things really start to get interesting. The

---

[301] Lipton, *Biology of Belief*, 107.

[302] Volume 5 of this series on Mental Illness will discuss the placebo effect as it relates to psychotherapy and pharmacology.

biochemical impact of the placebo effect potentially throws our whole model of disease into question.[303]

Although the medical model struggles to catch up with the reality that faith is powerful enough to influence a person's well-being, many scientists and physicians alike have realized the placebo's importance and are adjusting their medical practices.

Faith Enables Healing

The mind's ability to believe — to spiritually see a reality when no observable evidence exists (Hebrews 11:1-3) — directly affects and can alter the body when valid physiological diseases and mental struggles alike are present. Journalist Shirley Wang writes,

> Studies across medical conditions including depression, migraines and Parkinson's disease have found that supposedly inert treatments, like sugar pills, sham surgery and sham acupuncture, can yield striking effects. A 2001 study published in *Science* found that placebo was effective at improving Parkinson's disease symptoms at a magnitude similar to real medication. The placebo actually induced the brain to produce greater amounts of dopamine, the neurotransmitter known to be useful in treating the disease.[304]

Likewise, Dr. Rankin stresses that empathy and faith can control and alter the autonomic responses of the immune system. She says,

> Positive belief and nurturing care may also alter the immune system. People treated with placebos may experience boosts in immune function which results from flipping off the stress response and initiating the relaxation response. Placebos may also suppress the immune system. . . . Positive belief and nurturing care may also decrease the body's acute phase response, a type of inflammatory

---

[303] Rankin, *Mind over Medicine*, 11.

[304] Shirley S. Wang, "Why Placebos Work Wonders: From Weight Loss to Fertility, New Legitimacy for 'Fake' Treatments," *Wall Street Journal*, January 10, 2012, hhtp://online.wsj.com/article/SB1000142405297020472020457712887388864 71982.html.

response that leads to pain, swelling, fever, lethargy, apathy, and loss of appetite.[305]

Still another example of the power of faith to heal people from valid physical impairments is found in an article published in the prestigious *New England Journal of Medicine*. The article explains and summarizes the experiment and findings of orthopedic surgeon Dr. Bruce Moseley who specializes in knee surgeries.

Dr. Moseley conducted experiments for the purpose of discovering which surgical procedure brought about the most positive results for his patients. To test this theory, he divided his patients into three groups; one group received the standard procedure of shaving the damaged cartilage from the knee; the second group also received another regular treatment of flushing out the knee joint, and the third group was a placebo group that received a mock surgery including three small incisions and a video from someone else's surgery that the patient believed to be a live view of their own procedure.[306] His published findings were surprising to many who dismiss the power of the mind and faith:

> Our study found that outcomes after arthroscopic treatment are no better than those after a placebo procedure. This lack of difference suggests that the improvement is not due to any intrinsic efficacy of the procedures. Although patients in the placebo groups of randomized trials frequently have improvement, it may be attributable to either the natural history of the condition or some independent effect of the placebo.[307]

---

[305] Rankin, *Mind over Medicine*, 15.

[306] Lipton, *Biology of Belief*, 109.

[307] J. Bruce Moseley et al., "Controlled Trial of Arthroscopic Surgery for Osteoarthritis of the Knee," *New England Journal of Medicine* 347 (July 11, 2002): 81-88, http://www.nejm.org/doi/full/10.1056/NEJMoa013259#t=articleTop.

While this example of healing highlights the power of faith to heal valid physiological damage in the body, it also helps to establish faith as an essential element in physiological medicine. Moseley's study even convinced Dr. Lissa Rankin to reconsider her materialistic anthropology and begin to accept and understand mankind as being dualistic in nature:

> That [his study] was the first real evidence I collected that proved to me that a belief—something that happens solely in the mind—could alleviate a real, concrete symptom in the body. Dr. Moseley's study is what led me to research the placebo effect, the mysterious, powerful, reliably reproducible treatment affect some patient's experience when given fake treatment as part of a clinical trial.[308]

Another way in which faith has been observed through scientific methods to positively affect people's medical condition is found in fertility studies. Shirley Wang comments,

> Fertility rates have been found to improve in women getting a placebo, perhaps because they experience a decrease in stress. A recent randomized trial of women with polycystic ovarian syndrome found that 15%, or 5 of 33, got pregnant while taking placebo over a six-month period, compared with 22%, or 7 of 32, who got the drug—a statistically insignificant difference. Other studies have demonstrated pregnancy rates as high as 40% in placebo groups.[309]

Or consider the example of cancer patients being healed by unexplainable causes. The medical term *spontaneous remission* is often used by physicians to explain healing that occurs without the benefit of medicine and for no apparent reason. This phenomenon is quickly becoming recognized by a growing number of physicians and neuroscientists as an explainable result of the power of the mind to produce healing faith.[310] Dr. Lissa Rankin explains,

---

[308] Rankin, *Mind over Medicine*, 6.

[309] Wang, "Placebos Work Wonders."

[310] Ramachandran and Blakeslee, *Phantoms in the Brain*, 214-16.

> We know spontaneous, unexplainable remissions sometimes happen. Every doctor has witnessed them. We just shrug our shoulders and go on about our business, usually accompanied by a dull, unnerving sense of dissatisfaction because we can't explain the remission with logic.[311]

In a similar fashion, neuroscientist V.S. Ramachandran comments,

> As a student I was also taught that a certain proportion of incurable cancers — a very tiny fraction, to be sure — disappear mysteriously without any treatment and that "many a patient with a tumor pronounced malignant has outlived his physician." I still remember my skepticism when my professor explained to me that such occurrences were known as "spontaneous remissions." For how can *any* phenomenon in science, which is all about cause and effect, occur *spontaneously* — especially something as dramatic as the dissolution of a malignant cancer?[312]

Likewise, Dr. Lipton remarks,

> More baffling is the reality of terminal cancer patients who have recovered their lives through spontaneous remissions. Because such remissions are outside the bounds of conventional theory, science completely disregards the fact that they ever happened. Spontaneous remissions are dismissed as unexplainable exceptions to our current truths or simply misdiagnoses.[313]

What materialists cannot explain is often denied or set aside as an exception. If we accept dualism, however, then faith is a logical explanation for at least some spontaneous remissions. If we understand God's sovereignty, then God's merciful goodness and power over His creation must also be accepted.

While faith positively alters valid physical maladies and can even heal the body of physiological disease, faith is also essential for the mind's restoration. Take for example the secular construct of depression. Depression is another way to describe

---

[311] Rankin, *Mind over Medicine*, preface xvi.

[312] Ramachandran and Blakeslee, *Phantoms in the Brain*, 214-15.

[313] Lipton, *Biology of Belief*, 96.

deep sadness and hopelessness. Dr. Irving Kirsch, former
professor at Harvard University, explains,

> Whereas hopelessness is a central feature of depression, hope lies at
> the core of the placebo effect. Placebos instill hope in patients by
> promising them relief from their distress. Genuine medical
> treatments also instill hope, and this is the placebo component of
> their effectiveness. When the promise of relief instills hope, it
> counters a fundamental attribute of depression. Indeed, it is difficult
> to imagine any treatment successfully treating depression without
> reducing the sense of hopelessness that depressed people feel.
> Conversely, any treatment that reduces hopelessness must also
> assuage depression. So a convincing placebo ought to relieve
> depression.[314]

Though the placebo represents a false faith, it is still able to
provide the one who believes with hope.

Not only does the promise of hope remedy alleged
depression, but faith (the very substance of hope) also alters the
physical brain in those labeled as depressed. Dr. Lipton remarks,

> A California interior designer, Janis Schonfeld, who took part in a
> clinical trial to test the efficacy of Effexor in 1997, was just as
> "stunned" as Perez when she found out that she had been on a
> placebo. Not only had the pills relieved her of the depression that
> had plagued her for thirty years, the brain scans she received
> throughout the study found that the activity of her prefrontal cortex
> was greatly enhanced. (Leuchter, et al., 2002) Her improvements
> were not "all in her head." When the mind changes, it absolutely
> affects your biology.[315]

Faith has the power to physically alter the brain and the rest of
the body. Just as faith has the power to physically alter the brain
and heal the body, faith is also what truly remedies the mental
struggle and pain of deep sorrow and hopelessness that
secularists have labeled as depression.[316]

---

[314] Kirsch, *Emperor's New Drugs*, preface 3.

[315] Lipton, *Biology of Belief*, 111.

[316] Joe Dispenza, *You Are the Placebo: Making Your Mind Matter* (New York: Hay House, 2014), 7-9.

Additionally, faith is also foundational to the physician-patient relationship and directly affects patient outcomes. In the renowned journal, *The Lancet*, a study was published presenting clear evidence that a physician's own belief in his remedy and his communication to his patients of this faith directly affects patient outcomes.[317] If patients perceive a physician or a counselor to distrust his own methods or theory, then efficacy deteriorates. Dr. Lipton remarks, "By their words and their demeanor, physicians can convey hope-deflating messages to their patients, messages that are, I believe, completely unwarranted."[318] If patients feel hopeless or believe that they cannot trust their doctor, then outcomes will suffer. Ultimately, the person seeking help chooses what person and remedy is trustworthy. This faith has powerful effects, not only on the mind, but on the entire body.

Faith Enables Maladies

The "nocebo effect" or "nocebos" — terms used to identify faith that produces negative effects — are just as powerful as the placebo effect. The mind through faith can not only heal our physical maladies, it can also create or worsen valid physical illnesses. Former NIH researcher, Dr. Candace Pert explains,

> Blood flow is closely regulated by emotional peptides, which signal receptors on blood vessel walls to constrict or dilate, and so influence the amount and velocity of blood flowing through them from moment to moment. For example, people turn "white as a sheet" when they hear shocking news, or "beet red" when they become enraged. This is all part of the exquisite responsiveness of our internal system. However, if our flow can become chronically constricted, depriving the frontal cortex, as well as other organs, of vital nourishment, this can leave you foggy and less alert, limited in

---

[317] Richard H. Gracely et al., "Clinicians' Expectations Influence Placebo Analgesia," *Lancet* 325, no. 8410 (January 5, 1985): 43.

[318] Lipton, *Biology of Belief*, 112.

your awareness and thus your ability to intervene into the conversation of your body-mind, to make decisions that change physiology or behavior. As a result, you may become stuck—unable to respond freshly to the world around you, repeating old patterns of behavior and feeling that are responses to an outdated knowledge base.[319]

Likewise, Dr. Lipton asserts,

When the mind, through positive suggestion improves health, it is referred to as the placebo effect. Conversely, when the same mind is engaged in negative suggestions that can damage health the negative effects are referred to as the nocebo effect. In medicine, the nocebo effect can be as powerful as the placebo effect.[320]

The nocebo effect has broad meaning, but highlights the reality that a person's false faith, lack of faith, and negative faith can all directly affect his or her physical body in a negative way. One example of negative or false belief that alters the body is found in cases of *pseudocyesis*. Pseudocyesis is an observable physical phenomenon that occurs in women who believe that they are pregnant when they are not (oddly enough, it occurs in men too).[321] Convinced that she is pregnant, her body responds to her belief and fully changes as if she were carrying a baby.[322] Dr. Tarun Yadav explains,

In the case of pseudocyesis, i.e., phantom pregnancy, there is abdominal distention, enlargement of the breasts, enhanced pigmentation, cessation of menses, morning sickness and vomiting,

---

[319] Pert, *Molecules of Emotion*, 289.

[320] Lipton, *Biology of Belief*, 112.

[321] Ramachandran and Blakeslee, *Phantoms in the Brain*, 215-17, 218-220. See also Manny Alvarez, "Phantom Pregnancy: Imagining You Are Pregnant When You're Not," December 17, 2013, http://www.foxnews.com/health/2013/12/17/phantom-pregnancy-imagining-youre-pregnant-when-youre-not.html.

[322] Tarun Yadav, Yatan Pal Singh Balhara, and Dinesh Kumar Kataria, "Pseudocyesis Versus Delusion of Pregnancy: Differential Diagnoses to be Kept in Mind," *Indian Journal of Psychological Medicine* 34, no. 1 (Jan-Mar 2012): 82–84.

typical lordotic posture on walking, inverted umbilicus, increased appetite, and weight gain.[323]

In fact, researchers are studying pseudocyesis trying to figure out its cause. Psychiatrists Ibekwe and Achor remark,

> The etiology of pseudocyesis is still unclear despite considerable medical interest and speculations. Most of the currently accepted causal theories emphasize an interaction between psychological factors [the mind] and the reproductive system [the body], probably mediated by hormonal influences.[324]

Neuroscientist V.S. Ramachandran comments on how the mind produces these clear physical responses:

> It occurred to me that Pseudocyesis or phantom pregnancy might be an example of the kind of connections I was looking for [in mind-body medicine]. If the human mind can conjure up something as complex as pregnancy, what else can the brain do to or for the body? What are the limits to mind-body interactions and what pathways mediate these strange phenomena?[325]

Although Dr. Ramachandran denies the dual nature of humanity as Scripture sets forth in favor of a deterministic view and therefore uses *mind* and *brain* interchangeably, he does identify that the mind and faith are responsible for producing such physical changes. Psychiatrists Ibekwe and Achor later state that one of the most common causes of pseudocyesis is "an intense desire for, wish or fear of pregnancy, which results in pseudocyesis through complex neuroendocrine mechanisms."[326] Ultrasound has eliminated most cases of pseudocyesis in

---

[323] Ibid., 82–84.

[324] Perpetus Ibekwe and Justin Achor, "Psychosocial and Cultural Aspects of Pseudocyesis," *Indian Journal of Psychiatry* 50, no. 2 (Apr-Jun 2008): 112–16.

[325] Ramachandran , *Phantoms in the Brain, 215.*

[326] Ibekwe and Achor, "Aspects of Pseudocyesis," *Indian Journal of Psychiatry* 50, no. 2 (Apr-Jun 2008): 112–16.

developed countries as women can now observe that their womb is barren, and so their beliefs change.[327] But in third world countries where women often go without ultrasounds — such as in Africa — pseudocyesis is still very common and offers one example of the power of faith to negatively control the body.[328]

While even false faith — as demonstrated in placebo/nocebo studies — can bring healing, when it is realized to be false it can bring spiritual sickness to the one who believed. Proverbs 13:12 tells us that "hope deferred makes the heart sick, but a desire fulfilled is a tree of life." Scripture stresses that it is not merely faith that heals, but faith in what is true and sure. For spiritual healing to occur — something that we all desperately need and not just those who are labeled — we must turn to the only object of faith that can restore our minds to health. Ephesians 2:8-10 is one passage that shows the object of faith that is sure to alter our mind and even change our behavior. It says,

> For by grace you have been saved through faith. And this is not your own doing; it is the gift of God, not a result of works, so that no one may boast. For we are his workmanship, created in Christ Jesus for good works [behavior], which God prepared beforehand, that we should walk in them.

Grace is not a physical gift, but the spiritual reality of who Jesus Christ is and what He has done to provide a remedy that no one and nothing else can. While we were still sinners, Christ died on the cross to pay the price that God the Father requires to deal with our sin, our guilt, our fears, our sorrow, our poor relationships, our mental defects, and even death. But only by grace through faith can one receive this gift. To place one's faith in anything other than God's grace found in Jesus Christ to heal

---

[327] Ramachandran, *Phantoms*, 215-17, 218-20.

[328] Ibekwe and Achor, "Aspects of Pseudocyesis," 112–16.

the mind is to set one's self up for deeper heart sickness and inevitable destruction.

CONCLUSION

The overwhelming amount of available scientific research that qualifies as "exceptions" to the validity of the brain-dysfunction theory and the lack of empirical evidence to support it leave the secular construct of mental illness and biological psychiatry as unproven, invalid, and unreliable. The secular attempt to treat the mind through science and medicine — focusing on the nervous system and genetics — has not been a healing approach. Neo-Kraepelinian theory — which dominates the current construct — does not represent truth; it is merely an attempt to explain and view humanity apart from God and morality. Psychiatrists and other professionals who believe in materialism must hold to this theory in order to maintain control and relevance when it comes to the spiritual mind and our moral nature.

While many secularists have blindly accepted the brain-dysfunction theory, a growing number of honest scientists are discovering that humans are psychosomatic and that this perspective is the only valid and reliable way to define, understand, and approach humanity. In accepting the dual nature of mankind, scientists are able to understand that these coexisting natures work together to shape and influence who we are as people. They can observe and discern how the physical nature influences and affects the spiritual and mental states from observation and from Scripture. Though our physical nature influences our spiritual nature, physical impairments, damages, and defects never cause us to morally fail nor do they remove our responsibility to live wisely, to behave morally, and to love God and others.

Secularists continue attempts to define and study the mind within their scientific process, yet as we have noted, the mind is non-physical and not under the natural laws of science. Instead, the spiritual heart or mind is under the moral law of God and His authority, observable and discernible only through His wisdom (1 Chronicles 28:9). No matter the quantity of research that scientists conduct, answers about the human mind will always elude secularists who focus on physical and social sciences instead of the wisdom of God. It is this wisdom and grace alone that can truly heal and restore the mind and produce healthy, moral individuals and societies. Science — even neuroscience — will never be a tool to examine or approach the human mind.

Although science cannot examine or study the mind, it can observe the mind's effects on the body, but these observable effects invalidate the brain-dysfunction theory and support the reality of our psychosomatic nature. Whether it is through the study of psychoneuroimmunology, epigenetics, neuroplasticity, or the placebo and nocebo effects, the brain-dysfunction theory fails to account for the reality of faith and the power of the moral mind to control and change the physical body.

Not only does the brain-dysfunction theory fail to explain our mental, emotional, and behavioral problems, it also fails to account for the larger issues of life such as purpose, desire, intention, love/relationships, and faith to name a few. Science can observe the brain's connections, it can measure chemicals, it can evaluate genetic structures to an extent, and it can digitally scan and explore almost every region of the brain and understand where specific behaviors physically begin, but it cannot understand sadness, define desire, or explain the meaning of life:

> We know a lot about the mechanics of neurons and networks and brain regions — but we don't know why all those signals coursing

around in there mean anything to us. How can the matter of our brains cause us to care about anything? The meaning problem is not yet solved.[329]

Secularists wish to present faith and spirituality as unscientific, but being unscientific does not mean that they are not real. It simply means that the scientific process cannot be utilized to approach them. The secular perspective denies the existence of our spiritual heart though it still acknowledges the existence of desire, love, and meaning and hopelessly attempts to explain them through the physical body and the scientific process.

In truth, the brain-dysfunction and genetic theories fail to be valid working theories. Dr. Lipton explains,

> Remember the "dogma" that genes control biology? . . . Scientists, bent on establishing the validity of their truth, ignore pesky exceptions. The problem is that there *cannot* be exceptions to a theory; exceptions simply mean that a theory is not fully correct.[330]

Whether it be neuroplasticity, faith, psychoneuroimmunology, the dual nature of the nervous system, or the power of the mind to heal and physically alter the body, the overwhelming amounts of observable exceptions (empirical evidence) undermine the current theory that mental illness is a physiological matter. Humanity does not amount to amoral masses wandering through this dimension without responsibility. When understood through the lens of God's truth rather than through human speculation, one realizes that the human mind must be approached through the vehicle of faith rather than science or medicine. We are left understanding that though the physical body is relevant to our discussion, our physical natures are not the primary issue in matters of our

---

329 Eagleman, *Brain,* 33.

330 Lipton, *Biology of Belief,* 96.

mental anguish, impairments, and failures — what secularists often refer to as mental illnesses. In the same manner, medicine cannot provide genuine solutions that remedy the psyche and restore people to the image of God. God's grace alone can heal a person's mind and restore him to the image of His Creator.

BIBLIOGRAPHY

Abramson, John. *Overdosed America: The Broken Promise of American Medicine.* New York: Harper, 2005.

American Psychiatric Association. *Diagnostic and Statistical Manual of Mental Disorders: DSM-IV-TR.* Washington, DC: American Psychiatric Association, 2000.

American Psychiatric Association. *Diagnostic and Statistical Manual of Mental Disorders.* 5th ed. Washington, DC: American Psychiatric Publishing, 2013.

American Psychology Association. "*ICD* vs. *DSM.*" *Monitor on Psychology* 40, no. 9 (Oct 2009): 63.

Barkley, Russell A. *ADHD and the Nature of Self-Control.* New York: Guilford, 2005.

Begley, Sharon. *Train Your Mind, Change Your Brain.* New York: Ballantine Books, 2007.

Belden, Andy C., Deanna M. Barch, Timothy J. Oakberg, Laura M. April, Michael P. Harms, Kelly N. Botteron, and Joan L. Luby. "Anterior Insula Volume and Guilt: Neurobehavioral Markers of Recurrence after Early Childhood Major Depressive Disorder." *JAMA Psychiatry* 72, no. 1 (January 2015): 40-48.

Bentall, Richard. *Madness Explained: Psychosis and Human Nature.* New York: Penguin, 2003.

_____ . "Madness Explained: Why We Must Reject the Kraepelinian Paradigm and Replace It with a 'Complaint-Orientated' Approach to Understanding Mental Illness." *Medical Hypotheses* 66, no. 2 (2006): 220-33.

Berger II, Daniel. *Mental Illness: The Necessity for Faith and Authority*. Taylors, SC: Alethia International Publications, 2016.

_____ . *Mental Illness: The Reality of the Spiritual Nature*. Taylors, SC: Alethia International Publications, 2016.

Bettelheim, Bruno. *Freud and Man's Soul: An Important Re-Interpretation of Freudian Theory*. New York: Vintage Books, 1983.

Black, Edwin. *War Against the Weak: Eugenics and America's Campaign to Create a Master Race*. New York: Four Walls Eight Windows, 2003.

Boteach, Shmuel. *Moses of Oxford: A Jewish Vision of a University and Its Life*. London: Andre Deutsch Ltd, 1995.

Breggin, Peter. *Medication Madness: The Role of Psychiatric Drugs in Cases of Violence, Suicide and Murder*. St. Martin's Press, 2008.

_____ . *Toxic Psychiatry*. New York: St. Martin's Press, 1991.

Chan, Diana, and Lester Sireling. "'I want to be bipolar': A New Phenomenon." *Psychiatrist* 34, no. 3 (2010): 103–5.

Cherry, Kendra. "What is Humanistic Psychology?"
    http://psychology.about.com.

"'Complaint-Orientated' Approach to Understanding Mental
    Illness." *Medical Hypotheses* 66, no. 2 (2006): 220-33.

Coville, Walter, Timothy Costello, and Fabian Rouke. *Abnormal
    Psychology: Mental Illness Types, Causes, and Treatment.*
    New York: Barnes and Noble, 1960.

Darwin, Charles. *The Descent of Man, and Selection in Relation to
    Sex.* London: John Murray, 1871.

Detre, T. "The Future of Psychiatry," *American Journal of
    Psychiatry* 144, no. 5 (May 1987): 621-25.

Dispenza, Joe. *You Are the Placebo: Making Your Mind Matter.*
    New York: Hay House, 2014.

Doward, Jamie. "Psychiatrists under Fire in Mental Health
    Battle." *Guardian*, May 11, 2013.
    http://www.theguardian.com/society/2013/may/12/
    psychiatrists-under-fire-mental-
    health?CMP=share_btn_tw.

Dudley, M., and F. Gale. "Psychiatrists as a Moral Community?
    Psychiatry under the Nazis and its Contemporary
    Relevance." *Australian and New Zealand Journal of
    Psychiatry* 36, no. 5 (October 2002): 585-94.

Eagleman, David. *The Brain: The Story of You.* New York:
    Pantheon Books, 2015.

Ebert, Andreas, and Karl-Jürgen Bär. "Emil Kraepelin: A Pioneer of Scientific Understanding of Psychiatry and Psychopharmacology." *Indian Journal of Psychiatry* 52, no.2 (Apr-Jun 2010): 191-92.

Engstrom, Eric J. "'On the Question of Degeneration' by Emil Kraepelin (1908)." *History of Psychiatry* 18 (September, 2007): 389-98.

_____. "Psychiatric Observations on Contemporary Issues." *History of Psychiatry* 3 (1992): 253-69.

Fenwick, Peter. "Brain, Mind and Behaviour." *British Journal of Psychiatry* 163 (November 1993): 572.

Frances, Allen. *Saving Normal: An Insider's Revolt against Out-of-Control Psychiatric Diagnosis, DSM-5, Big Pharma, and the Medicalization of Ordinary Life*. New York: HarperCollins, 2013.

Freud, Sigmund. *Civilization and Its Discontents*. Translated by James Strachey. New York: Norton and Company, 1961.

Gijswijt-Hofstra, Marijke, Harry Oosterjuis, and Joost Vijselaar. *Psychiatric Cultures Compared: Psychiatry and Mental Health Care in the Twentieth Century*. Amsterdam: Amsterdam University Press, 2005.

Gray, J.P. "Insanity and Its Relations to Medicine." *American Journal of Insanity* 25 (1868): 145-72.

Green, Michael. *2 Peter and Jude: An Introduction and Commentary*. Vol. 18 of *Tyndale New Testament Commentaries*. Downers Grove, IL: InterVarsity, 1987.

Greenberg, Gary. *The Book of Woe: The DSM and the Unmaking of Psychiatry*. New York: Blue Rider Press, 2013.

Grinker, Roy R. "Psychiatry Rides Madly in All Directions." *Archives of General Psychiatry* 10 (1964): 228-37.

Grossman, Dave. *On Killing: The Psychological Cost of Learning to Kill in War and Society*. Rev. ed. New York: Back Bay Books, 2009.

Guthrie, W.K.C. *Aristotle: An Encounter*. Vol. 4 of *A History of Greek Philosophy*. New York: Press Syndicate of the University of Cambridge, 1981.

Hallowell, Edward M., and John J. Ratey. *Delivered from Distraction: Getting the Most out of Life with Attention Deficit Disorder*. New York: Ballantine Books, 2005.

Harris, Sam. *The End of Faith: Religion, Terror, and the Future of Reason*. New York: Norton and Company, 2005.

_____ . *Letter to a Christian Nation*. New York: Random House, 2006.

_____ . *The Moral Landscape: How Science Can Determine Human Values*. New York: Free Press, 2010.

Harrison, R.K. *Jeremiah and Lamentations: An Introduction and Commentary*. Vol. 21 of *Tyndale Old Testament Commentaries*. Downers Grove, IL: InterVarsity, 1973.

Hatfield, Agnes B. "The National Alliance for the Mentally Ill." *Community Mental Health Journal* 27, no. 2 (April 1991): 95-103.

Healy, David. *Let Them Eat Prozac: The Unhealthy Relationship between the Pharmaceutical Industry and Depression*. New York: New York University Press, 2004.

Hendriksen, William, and Simon J. Kistemaker. *Exposition of Paul's Epistle to the Romans*. Vol. 12–13. *New Testament Commentary*. Grand Rapids: Baker, 1953–2001.

Hergenhahn, B.R. *An Introduction to the History of Psychology*. South Melbourne, Victoria, Australia: Wadsworth Cengage Learning, 2009.

Hosenbocus, Sheik, and Raj Chahal. "A Review of Executive Function Deficits and Pharmacological Management in Children and Adolescents." *Journal of the Canadian Academy of Child and Adolescent Psychiatry* 21, no. 3 (2012): 223–29.

Hubble, Mark A., Barry L. Duncan, and Scott D. Miller, eds., *The Heart and Soul of Change: What Works in Therapy*. Washington, DC: American Psychological Association, 1999.

Jeffrey, C. Ray. "Biological Perspectives." *Journal of Criminal Justice Education* 4, no. 2 (1993): 303.

Jung, Carl G. *Dreams*. New York: Routledge Press, 2014.

Kandel, Eric. *In Search of Memory: The Emergence of a New Science of Mind*. New York: Norton Publishing Company, 2006.

Kidner, Derek. *Psalms 1–72: An Introduction and Commentary*. Vol. 15 of *Tyndale Old Testament Commentaries*. Ed. Donald J. Wiseman. Downers Grove, IL: InterVarsity, 1973.

King, D. Brett, Wayne Viney, and William Woody, *A History of Psychology: Ideas and Context*. New York, Pearson Education, 2009.

Irving Kirsch, *The Emperor's New Drugs: Exploding the Antidepressant Myth* (New York: Basic Books, 2011.

Klerman, Gerald L. "The Evolution of a Scientific Nosology." In *Schizophrenia: Science and Practice*. Edited by J.C. Shershow. Cambridge, MA: Harvard University Press, 1978.

Knezev, Sasha, and Gregory Smith. *American Addict*. Torrance, CA: Pain MD Productions, 2013.

Kraepelin, Emil. *Lectures on Clinical Psychiatry*. New York: Hafner, 1968 (reprint).

Kuhn, Thomas. *The Structure of Scientific Revolutions*, 3rd ed. Chicago: University of Chicago Press, 1996 first published in 1962.

Kutchins, Herb, and Stuart A. Kirk. *Making Us Crazy: DSM: The Psychiatric Bible and the Creation of Mental Disorders*. New York: Free Press, 1997.

Lange, John Peter, et al. *A Commentary on the Holy Scriptures: Jeremiah*. Bellingham, WA: Logos Bible Software, 2008.

Lapon, Lenny. *Mass Murderers in White Coats: Psychiatric Genocide in Nazi Germany and the United States*. Springfield, MA: Psychiatric Genocide Research Institute, 1986.

Laurence, William. "Surgery Used on the Soul-Sick," *New York Times,* June 7, 1937.

Leaf, Caroline. *Switch on Your Brain: The Key to Peak Happiness, Thinking, and Health.* Grand Rapids: Baker, 2013.

Lewontin, Richard. *Biology as Ideology: The Doctrine of DNA.* New York: HarperCollins, 1991.

Lieberman, Jeffrey A. *Shrinks: The Untold Story of Psychiatry.* New York: Little, Brown and Company, 2015.

Lipton, Bruce H. *The Biology of Belief: Unleashing the Power of Consciousness, Matter and Miracles.* New York: Hay House, 2005.

Lisanby, Sarah H. "Electroconvulsive Therapy for Depression," *New England Journal of Medicine* 357 (November 8, 2007): 1939-45.

Loemker, Leroy, ed. *Leibniz: Philosophical Papers and Letters.* Dordrecht, Netherlands: Reidel, 1969.

López-Muñoz, C Alamo, García, P., Molina, J.D., and Rubio, G. "The Role of Psychopharmacology in the Medical Abuses of the Third Reich: From Euthanasia Programs to Human Experimentation." *Brain Research Bulletin* 77, no. 6 (December 16): 388-403.

Maxmen, Jarold. *The New Psychiatrists.* New York: New American Library, 1985.

McKane, William. *Proverbs: A New Approach.* Philadelphia: Westminster, 1970.

McLaren, Niall. *Humanizing Psychiatry*. Ann Arbor, MI: Future Psychiatry Press, 2010.

_____ . "Kandel's 'New Science of Mind' for Psychiatry and the Limits to Reductionism: A Critical Review." *Ethical Human Psychology and Psychiatry* 10, no. 2 (July 1, 2008).

Menninger, Karl. *Bulletin of the Menninger Clinic* 53, no. 4 (July 1989): 350-52.

_____ . *The Vital Balance: The Life Process in Mental Health and Illness*. New York: Viking Press, 1963.

Meyer, J.E. "The Fate of the Mentally Ill in Germany during the Third Reich." *Psychology Medicine* 18, no. 3 (August 1988): 575-81.

Micale, Mark, and Roy Porter, eds. *Discovering the History of Psychiatry*. New York: Oxford University Press, 1994.

Miller, Henry George. "Psychiatry: Medicine or Magic?" *British Journal of Hospital Medicine* 22 (1970): 122-24.

Moll, Carl Bernhard. *The Psalms*. Translated and edited by Charles Biggs, John Forsyth, James Hammond, and Fred McCurdy. Vol. 9 of *Lange's Commentary on the Holy Scriptures*. Edited by Philip Schaff. 1872; reprint, Grand Rapids: Zondervan, n.d.

Mondimore, Francis Mark. *Bipolar Disorder: A Guide for Patients and Families*. 3rd ed. Baltimore: Johns Hopkins University Press, 2014.

Moncrieff, Joanna. *The Bitterest Pills: The Troubling Story of Antipsychotic Drugs*. London: Palgrave Macmillan, 2013.

Muller-Hill, Benno. *Murderous Science: Elimination by Scientific Selection of Jews, Gypsies, and Others. Germany 1933-1945*. Oxford: Oxford University Press, 1988.

Nikkel, Gina. "How to Fix the Broken Mental Health System: Ten Crucial Changes." *Psychiatric Times*, November 7, 2014. http://www.psychiatrictimes.com/career/how-fix-broken-mental-health-system-ten-crucial-changes#sthash.bWF2sHtk.dpu.

Oliver, Jeffery. "The Myth of Thomas Szasz." *New Atlantis* 13 (Summer 2006): 68-84.

Panksepp, Jaak, ed. *Textbook of Biological Psychiatry*. New York: John Wiley and Sons, 2004.

Patel, Vikram, Alistair Woodward, Valery L. Feigin, Kristian Heggenhougen, and Stella R. Quah, eds. *Mental and Neurological Public Health: A Global Perspective*. San Diego: Academic Press, 2010.

Pert, Candace B. *Molecules of Emotion: The Science behind Mind-Body Medicine*. New York: Scribner, 1997.

Petersen, Melody. *Our Daily Meds*. New York: Sarah Crichton Books, 2008.

Pierre, Joseph. "A Mad World." March 19, 2014. http://aeon.co/magazine/psychology/have-psychiatrists-lost-perspective-on-mental-illness/.

Popper, Karl. *Philosophy of Science: An Historical Anthology.* Edited by Timothy McGrew, Marc Alsperctor-Kelly, and Fritz Allhoff. New York: Wiley and Sons, 2009.

Porter, Roy. *Madness: A Brief History.* New York: Oxford University Press, 2002.

Powlison, David. "Is the Adonis Complex in Your Bible?" *Journal of Biblical Counseling* 22, no. 2 (2004): 42–58.

Proctor, Robert. *Racial Hygiene: Medicine under the Nazis.* Cambridge, MA: Harvard University, Press, 1988.

Ramachandran, V.S., and Sandra Blakeslee. *Phantoms in the Brain: Probing the Mysteries of the Human Mind.* New York: William Morrow and Company, 1998.

Rankin, Lissa. *Mind over Medicine: Scientific Proof that You Can Heal Yourself.* New York: Hay House Inc., 2013.

Restak, Richard. *The Brain has a Mind of Its Own: Insights from a Practicing Neurologist.* New York: Crown Publishers, 1991.

Reznek, Lawrie. *Evil or Ill?: Justifying the Insanity Defense.* New York: Routledge, 1997.

_____ . *Peddling Mental Disorder: The Crisis in Modern Psychiatry.* Jefferson, NC: McFarland, 2016.

Ropper, Allan H. "Two Centuries of Neurology and Psychiatry in the *Journal.*" *New England Journal of Medicine* 367 (July 5, 2012): 58-65.

Rose, Steve, and Hilary Rose eds. *Alas, Poor Darwin: The Case against Evolutionary Psychology*. London: Vintage Publishing, 2001.

Rosemond, John, and Bose Ravenel. *The Diseasing of America's Children: Exposing the ADHD Fiasco and Empowering Parents to Take Back Control*. Nashville: Thomas Nelson, 2008.

Rosenhan, David. "On Being Sane in Insane Places," *Science* 179, no. 4070 (January 19, 1973): 250-58.

Rush, Benjamin. "Observations Intended to Favour a Supposition That the Black Color of the Negroes Is Derived from the Leprosy." *Transactions of the American Philosophical Society* (1799): 4.

_____ . *Sixteen Introductory Lectures*. Philadelphia: Bradford and Innskeep, 1811.

Sacks, Oliver. *Hallucinations*. New York: Random House, 2012.

Sapolsky, Robert M. "The Frontal Cortex and the Criminal Justice System." *Philosophical Transactions of the Royal Society of London B: Biological Sciences* 359 (220): 1787-96.

Sargant, William. *Battle for the Mind: A Physiology of Conversion and Brainwashing*. New York: Harper and Row, 1971.

Sartorius, N., A. Jablensky, and R. Shapiro. "Two-Year Follow-up of the Patients included in the WHO International Pilot Study of Schizophrenia," *Psychological Medicine* 7, no. 3 (August 1977): 529-41.

Satel, Sally, and Scott Lilienfeld. *Brainwashed: The Seductive Appeal of Mindless Neuroscience*. New York: Basic Books, 2013.

Scheff, Thomas J. *Being Mentally Ill: A Sociological Theory*. Chicago: Aldine, 1966.

Schwartz, Jeffrey, and Rebecca Gladding. *You Are Not Your Brain: The 4-Step Solution for Changing Bad Habits, Ending Unhealthy Thinking, and Taking Control of Your Life*. New York: Penguin Group, 2011.

Schwarz, Allen. "Idea of New Attention Disorder Spurs Research, and Debate." *New York Times*, April 11, 2014.

_____ . "Still in a Crib, Yet Being Given Antipsychotics." *New York Times*, December 10, 2015.

Scull, Andrew. *Madness in Civilization: A Cultural History of Insanity from the Bible to Freud, from the Madhouse to Modern Medicine*. Princeton, NJ: Princeton University Press, 2015.

Seife, Charles. "How Drug Company Money Is Undermining Science." *Scientific American* 307, no. 6 (December 1, 2012).

Seligman, Martin *Learned Optimism: How to Change Your Mind and Your Life*. New York: Worth Publishers, 2006.

Sewell, Dennis. *The Political Gene: How Darwin's Ideas Changed Politics*. London: Picador, 2009.

Shorter, Edward. *A History of Psychiatry: From the Era of the Asylum to the Age of the Prozac*. New York: John Wiley and Sons, 1997.

Simon, Robert, and Liza Gold, eds. *The American Psychiatric Publishing Textbook of Forensic Psychiatry*. Washington, DC: American Psychiatric Publishing, 2010.

Spiegel, Alix. "The Dictionary of Disorder: How One Man Revolutionized Psychiatry." *New Yorker*, January 3, 2005. http://www.newyorker.com/magazine/2005/01/03/the-dictionary-of-disorder.

Starfield, Barbara. "Is US Health Really the Best in the World?" *Journal of the American Medical Association* 284, no. 4 (2000): 483-85.

Stip, Emmanuel. "Happy Birthday, Neuroleptics!" *European Psychiatry* 17 (2002): 115-19.

Stone, Alan. *Mental Health and Law: A System in Transition*. Rockville, MD: NIMH, 1975.

Stormer, John. *None Dare Call it Treason*. Cutchogue, NY: Buccaneer Books, 1964.

Strous, R. "Extermination of the Jewish Mentally-Ill during the Nazi Era: The 'Doubly Cursed.'" *Israel Journal of Psychiatry and Related Sciences* 45 (4) (2008): 247-56.

Sullivan, Harry Stack. *Interpersonal Theory of Psychiatry*. New York: W.W. Norton Company, 1953.

Szabo, Liz. "A Manmade Disaster: A Mental Health System Drowning from Neglect." *USA Today*, May 12, 2014.

Szasz, Thomas. "The Myth of Mental Illness." *American Psychologist* 15 (1960): 113-18.

———. *The Myth of Mental Illness: Foundations of a Theory of Personal Conduct*. New York: Harper Perennial, 2010.

———. *The Myth of Psychotherapy: Mental Healing as a Religion, Rhetoric, and Repression*. New York: Anchor Press, 1978.

———. *Psychiatry: The Science of Lies*. New York: Syracuse University Press, 2008.

———. *Schizophrenia: The Sacred Symbol of Psychiatry*. New York: Basic Books, 1976.

Tangney, June Price, and Ronda L. Dearing. *Shame and Guilt*. New York: Guilford, 2002.

Taylor, Robert L. *Finding the Right Psychiatrist: A Guide for Discerning Consumers*. New Brunswick, NJ: Rutgers University Press, 2014.

Torrey, E. Fuller. *The Death of Psychiatry*. New York: Penguin Books, 1975.

Valenstein, Elliot. *Blaming the Brain: The Truth about Drugs and Mental Health*. New York: Basic Books, 1998.

Van der Kolk, Bessel. *The Body Keeps the Score: Brain, Mind, and Body in the Healing of Trauma*. New York: Penguin, 2014.

Walker, Sydney. *A Dose of Sanity: Mind, Medicine, and Misdiagnosis*. New York: John Wiley and Sons, 1996.

Waltke, Bruce K. *The Book of Proverbs: Chapters 15-30. New International Commentary on the Old Testament*. Edited by R.K. Harrison and Robert L. Hubbard, Jr. Grand Rapids: Eerdmans, 2005.

Watkins, Alan, ed. *Mind-Body Medicine: A Clinician's Guide to Psychoneuroimmunology*. New York: Churchill Livingstone, 1997.

Watters, Ethan. *Crazy Like Us: The Globalization of the American Psyche*. New York: Free Press, 2010.

Weindling, Paul Julian. *Nazi Medicine and the Nuremberg Trials: From Medical War Crimes to Informed Consent*. New York: Palgrave MacMillian, 2004.

Whitaker, Robert. *Anatomy of an Epidemic: Magic Bullets, Psychiatric Drugs, and the Astonishing Rise of Mental Illness in America*. New York: Broadway Books, 2015.

Whitfield, Charles L. *The Truth about Mental Illness: Choices for Healing*. Deerfield Beach, FL: Health Communications, 2004.

William, Hirsch. *Religion and Civilization: The Conclusions of a Psychiatrist*. Charleston, SC: Nabu Press, 2010.

Wootton, Barbara. *Crime and the Criminal Law: Reflections of a Magistrate and Social Scientist*. Vol. 15. London: Stevens and Sons, 1981.

_____ . *Social Science and Social Pathology*. London: Allen and
     Unwin, 1968.

Wykes, Til, and Felicity Callard. "Diagnosis, Diagnosis,
     Diagnosis: Towards *DSM-5*." *Journal of Mental Health* 19
     no. 4 (2010).

Made in the USA
Columbia, SC
24 March 2018